CZECHMATE
Gerry Docherty and Bill Kinross

Cambridge University Press

CAMBRIDGE
LONDON   NEW YORK   NEW ROCHELLE
MELBOURNE   SYDNEY

ACT NOW PLAYS

Series editor: Andrew Bethell

Published by the Press Syndicate of the University of Cambridge
The Pitt Building, Trumpington Street, Cambridge CB2 1RP
32 East 57th Street, New York, NY 10022, USA
296 Beaconsfield Parade, Middle Park, Melbourne 3206, Australia

© Cambridge University Press 1982

First published 1982

Printed in Great Britain by
David Green Printers Ltd, Kettering, Northamptonshire

ISBN 0 521 28572 0 paperback

Performance
For permission to give a public performance of this printed
version of *Czechmate* please write to Permissions Department,
Cambridge University Press, The Edinburgh Building,
Shaftesbury Road, Cambridge CB2 2RU.

ABOUT THE PLAY

Events in the first half of 1968 had led the Czechoslovak people to feel that their country was really progressing towards a more democratic way of life under the leadership of Alexander Dubcek. But on 22 August the people of Prague woke up to find their streets over-run by Russian tanks. It was the end of the Prague spring and, overnight, all the leading Czechoslovak cities were under the control of invading troops.

No group felt more betrayed than the university students, whose protests had helped to bring down the hard-line ruling bureaucrats and give Czechoslovakia a glimpse of freedom. But what could they do to voice their outrage and defend their freedom? *Czechmate* is a play about how the young people of Prague reacted.

The play follows the experience of a group of student activists who lived through the protests, celebration and despair of those heady days. Their desperation culminates in one of them – Jan Palach – setting fire to himself in the centre of Prague.

It may be history but there is nothing dry about this play. By engaging its audience in the loves, ambitions and weaknesses of this group of ordinary young people, *Czechmate* puts life into events that remain all too topical. Dramatic actions may be shaping their futures, but the students still find much to joke about and plenty to worry and argue over.

Czechmate was originally presented as a full-scale musical, with fourteen original songs. Copies of the full musical score and permission to perform the musical version of *Czechmate* can be obtained from the authors at Alva Academy, Alva, Scotland. The lyrics of the songs included in the original production appear in ruled-off sections in the script, so that the text is clear to follow for a non-musical production or reading in class. Replacement dialogue for some of the songs is marked by a black line in the margin and should be omitted if the full musical version of the play is being used.

CHARACTERS

Male		*Female*	
PETER		ANNA	
JIRI	students at	LAURA	students at
VICTOR	Charles University,	MARGARITE	Charles University,
JAN	Prague	VALERIE	Prague
MARK		LISA a prostitute	

JOHAN   newspaper reporter
PAUL   newspaper reporter
EMIL   newspaper editor
DEAN   of philosophy faculty
ZARNAK   Police Commissioner
POLICE SERGEANT
POLICEMAN 1   (PC 1)
POLICEMAN 2   (PC 2)
VISCLAV   plain-clothes policeman
STARNAK   plain-clothes policeman
SOLDIER 1
SOLDIER 2
RUSSIAN COMMANDER
RUSSIAN MAJOR
RUSSIAN GUNNER
PRIEST

POLICEWOMAN   (WPC)
BREADWOMAN

Male or female
PEOPLE OF PRAGUE, ACADEMICS,
MILITARY PERSONNEL,
WAITERS/WAITRESSES,
POLICE

STAGE DIRECTIONS

There are two kinds of directions in this playscript. Those in **bold type** provide information that is essential to an understanding of what is happening in the play at that time. For a play-reading, these should be read by a separate reader.

Those in *italic type* are less essential stage directions and offer suggestions to assist with a production of the play on stage. In a reading they are best not read out as they will hamper the flow of the play, although those who are reading may find that some of these instructions offer help with the interpretation of their lines.

ACT ONE

SCENE 1   30 October 1967

Student refectory in the halls of residence of the Charles University of Prague: tables and chairs, a few posters, a canteen self-service bar. A group of students are gathered round a central table; one of them has just arrived.

PETER   Hey, Jiri, get me a coffee while you're there, will you?

JIRI   One sugar?

PETER   (*Softly*) Three.

ANNA   Three! (*Poking him rudely*) Do you know what you are doing to your system?

PETER   Ouch! It can't be worse than the harm you are doing to my system.

LAURA   A little sweetness never harmed any system, least of all this one.

JIRI   Here you are – rot your teeth.

PETER   Don't you start. (*Changing the subject*) How is your essay coming along – been at it all day?

JIRI   Yes, and I'm no further forward. Rumour has it that the Dean had an official visit from Zarnak complaining about the 'unhealthy elements'.

MARGARITE   Security Police? Again?

JIRI   Oh yes, they object to 'questionable intellectuals'.

PETER   Us? Intellectuals? Well, there's a compliment.

ANNA   'Course we're intellectuals, but we're loving with it.

JIRI   Give over, will you?

MARGARITE   I'm not so sure that we should be joking around like this. (*Looks around, worried.*) A word in the wrong ear can still be the end of a beautiful career.

PETER   Look, if we don't make a stand now, will we ever? When you have a career to protect, or a family, will you speak out then?

LAURA   It's true.

JIRI   Anyway, I hear there was a dreadful row; the Dean reckons we are heading for an almighty showdown – what with the drive for new approaches, and the old Party faithful.

LAURA   Reckons? Do you really think that the Secret Police will tolerate changes?

JIRI   Maybe. They rule by threat and fear – their threats, that's what they breathe, and our fear, that's what gives them strength – but people simply aren't as afraid as they used to be . . . Look at us . . . we dare to ask questions!

ANNA   Yes, to ourselves, and not always very loudly.

(**Enter** VICTOR **and** VALERIE, **two other students, out of breath. Their friends greet them.**)

VICTOR   (*Taking off his scarf and putting down his books*) So this is where you are; you weren't at the meeting!

JIRI   (*Distracted by the news*) What meeting? I've been over in the library.

PETER   Damnation – what happened? Where?

VICTOR   Over at the faculty hall.

VALERIE   (*Butting in only to praise Victor*) And Vic really showed them, he . . .

VICTOR   Hey, who's telling this story?

ANNA   I thought something was up.

VICTOR   Well, the meeting was kind of spontaneous, you know, but when we heard that the faculty had been threatened. . .

JIRI   Threatened? But who?

VICTOR   Yes, it seems the Dean has been warned that if the university cannot control its 'militants' steps will be taken to keep order.

PETER   Order! Huh! They mean brutalise anyone who stands in their way.

VICTOR   So, as the news spread round, we held a meeting.

VALERIE   And Vic said . . .

VICTOR   (*Firmly, almost unkindly*) I'm coming to that. (*Pause*) Anyway, a motion of confidence in the faculty was passed unanimously.

VALERIE   (*Excitedly*) Then Vic . . .

VICTOR   Then I demanded an end to academic restrictions, red tape, and these crummy facilities that always go wrong.

VALERIE   And the Secret Police!

VICTOR   And the Secret Police!

ANNA   Did you know that there have been four electricity blackouts in the last five days? That Board is so inefficient!

PETER   Did you really criticise the Secret Police?

VICTOR   Look, everyone . . . but everyone does it privately.

MARGARITE   But the danger? You could get into big trouble. Be very careful- they're bound to hear. Their little 'friends' are everywhere.

LAURA   But, haven't we heard all this so many times before? Shortages in the shops? Power failures? The Secret Police? I mean, one hour after a meeting – and do people even remember?

VICTOR   You could be right – a couple of beers and back to their books.

PETER   . . . Or their beds!

LAURA   Is that the depth of your philosophy? Two blankets?

PETER   *No* blankets.

ANNA   *(Putting on an air of great interest)* Well now!

VICTOR   Or mindless innuendo! What we need is . . .

(Suddenly all the lights go out. There is uproar.)

JIRI   NOT AGAIN!

LAURA   I don't believe it, and I've got hours of work to do this evening.

ANNA   That's five blackouts in six days.

VICTOR   See!

VALERIE   This is kind of romantic.

VICTOR   Romantic! Ouch!

ANNA   Take your hands off . . .

PETER   Sorry.

ANNA   No – not you – *you*! *(Slaps Jiri.)*

MARGARITE   Wait – I've got a torch.

VICTOR   Does no one listen? We've exams next week, but now – no lights, no heating. Does nothing in this bloody system work?

VALERIE   But Vic, what *can* we do?

VICTOR   We can organise ourselves and protest! Make them listen.

ANNA   How?

JIRI   Well, what *do* we do?

(Margarite switches on her torch. It is the only light.)

VICTOR   Come on, we're not taking this lying down. Let's all tell the people of Prague what's happening . . . it's the only way.

PETER   To the faculty hall?

VICTOR   To Wenceslas Square.

ALL   Right . . . Let's go!

LAURA   I'll never get that essay finished.

(They all go off. A spotlight reveals a POLICE SERGEANT, talking over the radio to a POLICE CONSTABLE.)

PC 1   *(Voice over radio)* Headquarters? There must be nearly a thousand of them . . . and they've got banners and placards . . . students with candles.

SERGEANT   Is it religious?

PC 1   I don't think so . . . no, no, it's not . . . it's something to do with an electricity supply failure.

SERGEANT   Well break it up!

PC 1   There are hundreds . . . thousands of them.

SERGEANT   I'm sending out reinforcements . . . are they armed?

PC 1   No . . . but bloody noisy.

SERGEANT   Stay with them . . . we're on our way. The Deputy Commissioner is coming down. If it's a showdown they want, a showdown they can have.

PC 1   Guns?

SERGEANT   No, batons . . . and give them a proper taste of law and order.

(A single spotlight reveals Victor on a bare stage. During the song, students move behind him in sequence.)

Song: Light Up Your Life

VICTOR   Now they've put out the lights,
We're supposed to take fright,
Crawl back into our rooms;
We're just empty heads,
Who ought to be in bed,
Not speaking our minds, they presume.
Well, are you gonna make it,
Or lie down and take it,
Let them trample all over us?
Are we in the right,
Is it worth a stand-up fight,
Or don't you want any fuss?

ALL (*Chorus*)   Light up your life, face up to the strife,
Feel proud enough to cry stop!
If it's getting you down,
Let's march on the town:
We'll protest now until we drop.
The choices are stark!
Either sit in the dark
Or get off your backs and join in.
If we keep quiet now,
We may as well bow
To their wishes and simply give in.

(*Victor moves across the stage to meet a group of* ACADEMICS.
During the following verse, the DEAN *tries to get Victor to sing
more quietly, since what he is saying is dangerously outspoken.*)

VICTOR   Excuse me now, Prof,
Do you have to doff
Your cap to the Communist way?
If you happen to think
That this country will sink,
Are you allowed so to say?
Can you honestly teach
The dogmas *they* preach?
Or are you caught fast in a trap?
Is telling the truth
Somewhat worse than uncouth?
Are you left feeling a sap?
Well then . . .

ALL *(Chorus)*   Light up your life, etc.

(Victor moves across the stage to a group of WORKERS *and*
PEOPLE OF PRAGUE.)

VICTOR   Does the factory hand
Think that life is so grand,
His pay a rich reward?
Are the hours he works fair,
Or must he take care
Lest the manager's not in accord?
Does his wife have a voice,
Or much of a choice,
When she tries to buy him his clothes?
Do the shops have much food?
If they do, is it good?
Be honest, can we ever know?
Why then . . .

ALL *(Chorus)*   Light up your life, etc.

*(Victor moves to the other side of the stage to a fourth
group - the* MILITARY.)

VICTOR   Though you're called up to serve,
Have you got the nerve
To think of your country first?
Would an act of defiance
Ruin the Moscow alliance,
Would Brezhnev's blood vessels burst?
Think of the past:
Can tyranny last?
Do you want to remain suppressed?
Can you think of a curse
That could ever be worse
Than this - a nation depressed?

ALL *(Chorus)*   Light up your life, etc.

*(Placards appear and the assembled cast moves back and forth
in procession, ending in a defiant posture at the end of a repeat
of the chorus.)*

**(The baton-swinging POLICE emerge and wade into the student
ranks. Victor and two other students are arrested.)**

SCENE 2   The Police Commissioner's office in central Prague. The only person on stage is the Police Commissioner, ZARNAK. He is sitting behind a big desk, on which is set a single telephone and a single desk photograph of Novotny.*

ZARNAK   (*On telephone*) Yes, sir, my men have the situation well under control . . . 'unusual'? (*Pause*) Sir, the word is 'unique' – I've never heard of the like . . . here, in Prague . . . a *demonstration!* Never . . . it has never happened before, and believe you me, it will not happen again. Dangerous? Well, we must make sure that these student upstarts are put in their place. (*Pause*) Exactly, make an example of a few, and the rest will fall in line . . . quite . . . this is the trouble with people who think, they think they know better, especially the young ones. I blame these Western influences, and a lack of discipline at home and . . . yes (*pause*), yes, of course, Minister. I will keep you informed. (*Disgust registering in his voice*) Goodbye. (*He looks at the phone, slams it down and shrugs his shoulders.*) That's the trouble with politicians, they like to hear themselves speak . . . but not anyone else.

(He is interrupted by a POLICEWOMAN, with back-combed hair, holding a clipboard.)

WPC   Excuse me, Commander, the task-force leader at the university wants to know if you want wholesale arrests.

ZARNAK   (*Looks perplexed. He has never been in such a predicament before.*) Have we got the resources? Is it worth it? We *must* make an example of some of them. What a disgraceful thing, and here in Prague too! Tell him to lift the ringleaders, if that is possible, and make the message clear: NO MORE DEMONSTRATIONS! (*Thumps the desk.*) I've had the Minister of the Interior on the phone, you know, bloody students!

---

* Novotny was the hard-line Moscow-backed communist leader of Czechoslovakia in 1967.

WPC   Three of those arrested in the streets are downstairs now, sir. One whimpering he had nothing to do with the riot, one extremely tight-lipped, and one fool promising that 'our time will come soon.'

ZARNAK   (*Smiling cruelly*) Really? How stupid! Bring them up; I'd like to have a word with them.

WPC   Very good, sir.

(**WPC goes off. Zarnak picks up the phone and dials.**)

ZARNAK   (*In a very commanding manner*) Visclav? I want you and Starnak in my office immediately.

(**He slams down the phone, opens a file and pretends to be working. VISCLAV and STARNAK, plain-clothes policemen, enter – obviously henchmen.**)

VISCLAV   Sir.

(**Zarnak ignores them for about five seconds, looks up, scowls and snaps them into position on either side of his desk. The three students: VICTOR, MARK and JAN, are hustled into his office.**)

ZARNAK   Stand up straight, you impertinent slob.

VICTOR   It's not too easy to stand up straight when your collar bone feels broken and your kidneys are bruised to pulp.

ZARNAK   You are a medical student?

VICTOR   No.

ZARNAK   Then stop kidding yourself – you'll survive (*pause*), perhaps, should we so decide. (*Pause*) But not for long if you keep trying to subvert the interests of the State.

VICTOR   The interests of the Party.

ZARNAK   (*Slapping him across the face*) Let me guess, you are the one who has been threatening my men: 'our time will come', I believe! You are either extremely foolhardy or exceedingly brave. What a stupid thing to say if you can't do anything about it – or can you? (*Pause*) You are a spy? Who recruited you – the CIA? You are in league

with others . . . with outsiders? We will check . . . of that
you can be certain.

VICTOR You *know* we are not. You know we are just young
people who want to see our nation do well – work under
normal conditions – not fester in this . . .

(Zarnack punches Victor in the stomach.)

ZARNAK Young man, bravery I admire, stupidity I cannot tolerate.
The margin between the two is a very narrow one. If you
wish to be a martyr, so be it, but smart remarks within
these four walls will get you nowhere. Tell me, what does
your father do?

VICTOR This has got nothing to do with . . .

ZARNAK It has to do with what I say it has to do with – your
mother? You have perhaps brothers and sisters who one
day hope to go to university? Pity, if they have to leave
school (*to audience*) not quite up to standard. (*Swings back
to Victor.*) Our arms reach everywhere.

VICTOR But . . .

ZARNAK (*Angrily*) NO BUTS! We will NOT BE INTIMIDATED BY THIS
IDEOLOGICAL SUBVERSION from the CAPITALIST WEST! Look
at you – a hooligan – hair too long, unwashed no doubt,
full of bullshit.

ZARNAK (*Moves on to Jan, provoking him.*) And what have you got to
say for yourself?

(Jan stares at him with cold hatred. He says nothing.)

ZARNAK Have you lost your tongue, boy? Speak!

JAN What do you want us to say? 'Sorry! We didn't mean to
complain . . .'

(Zarnak slaps him unceremoniously and moves on.)

MARK I wasn't . . . hadn't anything to do with the . . .

ZARNAK You attend the university?

MARK   (*Stammering, showing obvious fear*) Yes.

ZARNAK   You know these two?

MARK   (*Dropping his head*) N-n-no

(*Victor and Jan both look at him in disgust.*)

ZARNAK   (*Laughing*) HA! You're a pathetic liar, but at least you know your place. (*Pause*) Take this one away – is he charged with anything? (*The police shake their heads.*) Then let him go. (*Walks to his desk, spins round and begins.*) As for you two, let me make myself perfectly clear. Should either of you cross my path, then you will never, NEVER, have cause to do so again. You will NOT be students, you will not be taking up attractive jobs. Next time – if there is a next time – will be the last time. Understand?

(He hits Victor.)

Understand? (*Victor grunts.*)

Understand?

(He hits Jan.)

JAN   (*In pain*) Yes.

ZARNAK   Take them away – put them in the cells!

(The students are hauled out, leaving Zarnak to shake his head in considerable disbelief.)

(*To audience*) If only they could hear themselves. Endless chatter: 'Down with this', 'That's all wrong', 'We want freedom', 'We want everything' . . . and always 'now'. Oh yes, and 'All those over fifty are senile or deranged'. Never mind that we brought them up, looked after them, cared for them. They take all that for granted and despise us for the occasional reminder that they've got a lot to learn. And I, for one, do not go along with the misguided liberals who say that they are too young to do real harm. They certainly do not know exactly what it is they want, but these open-ended requests: 'We want

. . .', 'Give us . . .', all add up to rebellion, if you are fool enough to allow it. If you threaten the peace, if you disturb the happy balance we have built up over the years, who knows where it could lead? They need to be contained. That's my job . . . and I shall not shrink from my responsibility, whatever the press or Party may say. The hard line is the only line. If we were soft enough to show any weakness . . . then be sure, the whole fabric of our society would be at risk.

Song: Try to Tell a Teenager

ZARNAK   If only youth could hear itself
Repeat those clichéd cries:
'Down with this', 'That must go',
Brings tears to a glass eye.
Every State decision's wrong,
The old ways must be changed,
And all those over fifty
Are senile or deranged.

You bring them up as best you can,
Give them all you've got,
Try to make the system safe,
And they reject the lot.
Try to tell a teenager
No more than common sense,
And watch them stand and look at you
As if you are dense.

It's said that youth is innocent,
Too young to do real harm,
But dreams don't make reality:
That's wherein lies the charm;
And what is it they really want?
More jobs or cash or fame?
The trouble is they never know
But demand just the same.

Each year we hear the age-old pleas:
'We want', 'Give us', 'Resign',
With words like 'Rights' and 'Freedom',
Suggestions I decline.
We have our job to guard the State
From dangerous unrest;
At times it's not too pleasant
But what we have is best.

It's my responsibility
To keep us free from strife,
Ferret out the dissidents,
Remove them from street life.
I don't want praise or even thanks
From Party or the press;
The hard line works, we must stand firm,
Weakness leads to unrest.

(He moves back to his desk, shaking his head, and picks up the phone again.)

ZARNAK   Visclav, make sure that those two are kept awake all night- do the 'are you working for the CIA?' routine. Put the fear of God into them . . . don't be impertinent, I know there is no God- it's just a phrase!

(He slams down the phone.)

SCENE 3   **A street café in the main square in Prague. The girls from the university are having a coffee, worried about the night before. The café is the haunt of a cross-section of Prague's population, especially the press. A WAITRESS hovers in the background.**

MARGARITE   (*In exasperation*) You're sure you've checked everywhere?

VALERIE   (*Sobbing*) Of course I have- he didn't get back to the halls: he hasn't been home.

ANNA   Maybe he stayed with Alexus or Jan, or took refuge somewhere.

VALERIE   (*Getting angrier*) Where? I just know he was arrested. Oh why didn't I stay by his side?

LAURA   Valerie, give yourself a good shake-your imagination will run away with itself. Victor isn't a baby!

(**Two reporters, JOHAN, a young man, and PAUL, much older and much more cynical, enter.**)

VALERIE   (*Rushing out of her seat*) Johan-Johan has *your* paper any information about those who were arrested last night? Was . . . was Victor caught?

JOHAN   Calm yourself, Valerie, this thing came like a bolt out of the blue. The Police certainly over-reacted-cracked a few heads-but I don't think it will come to much.

PAUL   Serves them right-demonstrations in the street. Doesn't anyone remember Hungary? This nonsense will have to stop before people *really* get hurt.

JOHAN   Don't be such a pessimist-this *is* 1967.

LAURA   And if we don't complain, who will-you? You only write what the Party wants to read!

PAUL   We write what we can, without putting the whole of society at risk.

ANNA   What society? What risk? Is this worth keeping? This magnificent stagnation, this Police State? Is your foolish brain fouling up? Whose side are you on anyway?

PAUL   Whose side? My side, my dear, my side. I've long learned that the one man I can trust is-me.

JOHAN   OK, OK. You wait and see, it will be the Writers' Congress which takes up these wrongs. We do more to question the State and seek reform than anyone else-so lay off the press, eh!

VALERIE   (*Standing alone on the other side of the stage, realises that she has ceased to be the centre of attention and cries aloud*) Victor . . . Oh Victor-I know he's dead.

LAURA   (*Sarcastically*) More likely dead drunk.

VALERIE   (*Moving menacingly towards Laura*) How dare you, he's very brave-and he cares about his country.

LAURA   (*Aside*) More than he cares about you.

ANNA   (*Moving in fast to avert a nasty scene*) Girls, please, come on. (*She links arms between them. Margarite grabs the bags, etc.*)

JOHAN   (*Shouting across as they leave*) If he does turn up, where will you be?

VALERIE   At the halls. (**Laura, Anna and Valerie go off.**)

PAUL   (*Shaking his head scornfully*) Idiots!

JOHAN   Let them be . . . (*Pauses and moves closer to Paul.*) What did the Editor think of the demonstration?

PAUL   He knows my views – we didn't even discuss the stupidity. (*A waitress comes over.*) Two coffees, please.

JOHAN   (*Getting excited*) I don't know – who would have thought to see a student demonstration? And I know for a fact that the Writers' Congress is spoiling for a fight with that ignorant Culture Minister, Hendrych.

PAUL   (*Almost absent-mindedly*) Danger.

JOHAN   Come off it. Look how the students feel – they're not alone.

PAUL   Son, I survived the Nazis, I even remember further back to the old Austrian monarchy, but you can't change this. Novotny will *always* have his way. He's backed by Moscow. (*Pause*) I was in Budapest in 1956, you know. You don't forget the sight of tanks blasting away at point-blank range, pummelling at a few snipers in a city-centre block of flats, or bodies rotting in the rain as Soviet troops 'liberate' a people who are simply trying to free themselves. I don't want to see that here, now.

JOHAN   But it won't be like that – no one's talking about breaking away from Russia.

(**Enter a PRIEST, who sits at a table behind the two journalists.**)

Good morning, Father . . . and we, the writers in Czechoslovakia, must *be* involved in change. If we don't back those journalists who are telling the truth, what then? We *have* to be involved.

PAUL   We do not . . .

(Enter LISA, a high-class prostitute.)

Well, hello Lisa. How's business? Had a good night?

LISA   Good night? Good night? You must be joking with all that noise – the police blowing whistles and chasing students – huh! What a disgusting way to behave; whoever heard of such nonsense? How can an honest lady survive?

PRIEST   Honest lady? To what depths has our language deteriorated?

LISA   Charming . . . such charity.

JOHAN   (*Butting into the confrontation*) So you had a rough night too? It seems quite a few did.

LISA   (*Looking around to see who is listening*) Still, I think things are moving in the right direction.

(Enter VICTOR and JAN, both a bit dazed but obviously well.)

PAUL   Don't you start . . . oh no . . . here come the heroes of the new revolution.

JOHAN   (*Rising to greet them*) Victor, are you OK? And your friend?

VICTOR   (*Introducing his comrade*) Jan . . . yes, yes . . . we've been kept up all night, but the bully boys really weren't very impressive.

LISA   You sure you are all right, boys? I could discount some sympathy if you need attention.

PAUL   (*Pushing in*) You *were* arrested?

VICTOR   Yes.

PAUL   And they . . . let you out?

VICTOR   Obviously.

PAUL   (*Scratching his head*) Well, that does surprise me. Something's up.

JOHAN   They can't be too confident that the Party will fully back them up . . . and the Police did over-react.

LISA   See, there is hope.

PAUL   Hope? Woman – act your age!

LISA   (*Strongly*) To be without hope – that is the loneliest way of all.

Song: Hope

LISA   Hope, the budding spring flower as it rushes out to bloom,
And the cheery-faced young schoolboy barging out from the classroom,
Grows again inside our hearts, fills our every waking hour,
Letting dreams of how it might be warm our senses with false power;
While our heartbeat quickens, daily, and our step has raised its pace,
And there's sparkle in your bright eyes, a flush upon your face.

May it be so, may it be so – don't stop now. Go the whole way,
Make your motto be: 'Tomorrow begins more than just a day.'
Hear the people, hear their clamour, they just want to have their say,
Now has come, forget the strains that only held back yesterday.
May it be so, may it be so – don't stop now. Go the whole way,
Make your motto be: 'Tomorrow begins more than just a day.'

Faith, they say, moves mountains and its power is ever deep,
And the strength it gives conviction can never be bought cheap;
It's the fire that fills the belly, though there be no other food,
The voice that brooks no question, as if any question could,
And its roots lie in the knowledge that, yes, of course, we're right,
It's the power that leads us onwards; it's why we'll win our fight.

May it be so, may it be so, etc.

VICTOR   Well done, that was really nice-but haven't I heard it somewhere before?

LISA   Well-it's been doing the rounds of the folk clubs.

PAUL   Romantic rubbish.

PAUL   (*To Victor*) You I know, but who is your friend?

VICTOR   This is Jan, he's doing philosophy, too.

PAUL   Mug.

LISA   You are so nice to people-you must practise hard.

PAUL   I work hard-and during the day-so I'll leave you to dream on. Come on, Johan.

JOHAN   (*Turning to Victor as he prepares to leave*) Listen, Vic, I think that there will be a vacancy at the paper soon-interested?

VICTOR   (*Enthusiastically*) Interested? Of course!

JOHAN   Good. Don't build your hopes up, but I'll do what I can. Goodbye.

VICTOR   (*Still surprised by the offer*) Goodbye.

JAN   What a break that would be, Vic. It's what you've always wanted. Let's hope it comes off.

VICTOR   Sure.

LISA   Oh no! Time to move on.

(**Enter Anna and Laura, led by the over-excited Valerie. Behind them come** JIRI **and** PETER. **They rush on, delighted to see Victor; only Peter talks to Jan.**)

VALERIE   Oh Victor, Victor. I thought you were in jail, I thought . . .

VICTOR   It's not your strong point, Val . . . thinking never was.

ANNA   What happened?

PAUL   Are you all right?

JIRI   (*Almost disappointed*) You weren't beaten up?

VALERIE   Oh! Were you tortured? (*Sits down.*)

VICTOR   Would you listen to this, Jan. They want to canonise us already. We're all right (*stressing the point*). Zarnak has expressed a personal interest in our future.

ALL   ZARNAK!

VICTOR   (*Nodding emphatically*) Zarnak. But don't worry, we really are all right.

VALERIE   (*Taking Victor's arm*) I'll take you home.

VICTOR   Just let me get some rest, Val. OK?

VALERIE   (*Disappointed*) OK.

PETER   The Dean of the faculty wants to see everyone involved in last night's demonstration. He wants to find out exactly what happened. I think he's preparing a formal protest.

VICTOR   Good for him! I'll . . . (*Looking at Jan*) No, *we'll* go there first while we still look worn out.

VALERIE   Right, I'll come with you and . . .

VICTOR   (*Emphatically*) NO! I think it would be better if Jan and I went alone, otherwise we might not get enough sympathy.

VALERIE   (*Dejectedly*) OK – I'll come over later.

VICTOR   (*Rising*) Right, come on Jan.

PETER   We'll see you back at the halls, then – cheerio.

(Assorted farewells, as Victor and Jan leave. The others sit down. Valerie is looking very starry-eyed towards Victor's exit.)

LAURA   Well, Val, he's alive, he's safe, and you can relax.

VALERIE   Mmmmmm.

ANNA   Now look, we've just been through the 'worried-to-death-and-I-don't-think-I-can-live-one-more-hour' routine – all for nothing, I might add, and the big lump is off to crawl to the Dean.

VALERIE   Anna!

ANNA   So let's just calm down and have a coffee.

PETER   (*Waving his hands in front of a glazed Valerie*) I don't think she hears much.

JIRI   It's love.

LAURA   It's worship.

ANNA   But didn't you know? He's a hero.

VALERIE   He *is*!

JIRI   He is?

LAURA   I'm not even sure he's human.

PETER   True . . . he just glides across the floor, doesn't he, Val?

VALERIE   Huh!

JIRI   He's not much good at walking on water . . . he nearly drowned last week in the swimming pool.

VALERIE   He did not. He's a good swimmer.

ANNA   But of course.

LAURA   (*Suggestively*) Is there anything he's not wonderful at?

VALERIE   Wouldn't you love to know?

JIRI   It must be boring . . .

VALERIE   Boring?

PETER   Yes, being so good at everything . . . so wonderful . . . I'm glad I'm not wonderful.

ANNA   You do think you are perfect, though?

PETER   Naturally.

LAURA   Ah . . . for a male ego . . . and they say women are vain.

Song: He's a Hero

LAURA, ANNA, PETER, JIRI	There's a wild gleam in her eye, Every line ends with a sigh, She sees just him, no one else gets through. Does he walk or does he glide? Oh to be there by his side: A God to her, though merely man to you. Do you think she's maybe dim To see anything in him? Perhaps we ought to take her to the vet. Yes, a doctor is no use; She'd only give him mad abuse, For there's really only one man in her life.
ALL *(Chorus)*	And he's a Hero, can't you understand? A Hero, isn't it just grand? Everything he does, he does with style, For he's her Hero, Mr Always Right. A Hero, such a lovely sight; I wonder what it's like to be so fine; For me I'm glad he'll never be all mine.
LAURA, ANNA, PETER, JIRI	Now Heroes they win races, Save hopeless legal cases, Often score the final winning goal; Heroes never hit the dirt, They always sport a bright clean shirt, Success is naturally their biggest role; They're the ones the crowds all cheer, Toast in vodka or in beer, They even end up written into song; Of course they win when all seems lost, Never stop to count the cost, Now where on earth do you think she went wrong?
ALL *(Chorus)*	And he's a Hero, etc.
VALERIE	You can say just what you like, Call me names of every type, But I don't think that I will ever care. When my Hero's in the flat, My mind seizes just like that, It hazes into heaven when he's near; I fear my heart may really blow

All its fuses, don't you know,
A Hero makes your heart beat double-quick;
You can keep your jealousies,
Yes, my Hero's all for me,
The way you go on's positively sick, for . . .

ALL (*Chorus*)   He's a Hero, etc.

SCENE 4   **March 1968**

The boys' room at the university: sparsely furnished but
comfortable. Books are strewn around. Posters on the wall. An
imported Beatles album is lying propped up against a record
player. A door on the right leads to other rooms. PETER is
reading the paper. JIRI and LAURA are writing at a table. ANNA
is lying on the floor by the settee.

PETER   (*Shaking with excitement*) Listen! Listen to this: 'The
Minister of the Interior has made a formal apology to the
students of Prague for the maltreatment of student
demonstrators by Police on 30 October 1967.'

JIRI   (*Excitedly*) Wow! That's one to chalk up for freedom.
What does it say?

PETER   Oh, it's not much of an apology, really- more of a
justification. But surely that's a sign of the times.

ANNA   All these dismissals inside the Party- I can't believe all
that's happening.

LAURA   They say this new guy, Dubcek, is really sweeping away
the old fogies.

PETER   Mind you, we still have a long way to go before all the
wrongs of the last twenty years are put right.

JIRI   Don't get carried away.

(Enter VALERIE with her hair wrapped in a towel, rubbing her
eyes.)

VALERIE   Has anyone seen the electric fire?

PETER   (*Pointing to one side of the settee*) There it is, and you'd better *not* make too much mess. Hey! I almost forgot, have you heard the news?

VALERIE   News? What news?

PETER   They've publicly apologised for arresting Victor.

VALERIE   (*Showing great interest*) What? Is his name in the paper?

JIRI   (*Mocking her*) Oh yes, headline news: 'Victor-We're Sorry!'

VALERIE   Where? Let me see.

ANNA   (*Annoyed at her friend's gullibility*) Oh for goodness sake! That girl! Go away and electrocute yourself with that fire, and try not to singe your hair this time.

(Valerie stomps off.)

PETER   You lot are quite cruel to her sometimes. I think you are jealous.

LAURA   Jealous! Us! You must be kidding!

(*Noise of door banging*)

PETER   Sober up-this must be Victor.

(Enter VICTOR, briskly. He takes off his coat, smiles without saying anything, nods to everyone, and sits smugly in the middle of the settee. Everyone looks at him. No one has yet spoken. They look at eath other.)

JIRI   Well?

VICTOR   Yes, thank you.

ANNA   Come off it, Vic. Something's up . . . playing hard to get, are we?

VICTOR   I never said a word.

LAURA   News of more changes? Little else seems to register with you these days. A new TV programme?

VICTOR   Well, now that they have virtually abolished censorship it seems that the Czechoslovakian press has decided to employ one of the country's leading young writers.

JIRI   (*Hitting him with a pillow*) You've got the job–you jammy beggar–you've got the job.

(Enter Valerie, hair in curlers.)

VALERIE   What's up? Who's got a job? Victor? (*A scream of delight*) Oh that's marvellous.

(She tries to give him a kiss; he ducks, and she falls right over the side of the settee.)

PETER   You've really got a job as a journalist?

VICTOR   Yep!

VALERIE   (*Slinking closer to him on the settee*) Oh Victor.

LAURA   Will you still mix with us now that you have reached the dizzy heights of newsboy?

VICTOR   (*Not liking the tone of this conversation*) Give over will you?

Song: Mr Newsman

PETER, JIRI, LAURA, ANNA

Hey, Mr Newsman, write us a story:
Front page car crash, picture that's gory;
Hey, Mr Newsman, is it too hot to handle:
Government foul-up, political scandal?
Hey Mr Newsman, rake in the dirt,
Make a kiss on the cheek look a villainous flirt.
Hey, Mr Newsman, will you abuse, man, the power of the
    press?
Careful as you go, man, can't be the cause of the Party's
    distress.

How did you do it, did you have to work hard?
Or did you take the easy way with the Party's magic card?
Have you sold out all your friends, do we now all have to bow?
Will you report our meetings? Tell us right now.

Hey, Mr Newsman, what are your views, man?
Do you write for the people or for the State?
Hey, Mr Newsman, why hound the Jews, man,
Or will the Editor simply create?
Hey, Mr Newsman, you'll take abuse
If you don't write it down just the way that they want;
Take half a lie, add some fact, if you try
You can twist anything–but please don't.

How did you do it, etc.

Hey, Mr Newsman, don't you confuse, man,
The needs of the people with the Party chiefs.
Make sure you use, man, the right kind of views, man,
Promotion comes with accepted beliefs.
Hey, Mr Newsman, it must amuse, man,
To know what they've really got to hide:
A prisoner falls from the seventeenth floor,
Of course, it must be suicide.

How did you do it, etc.

(*Victor protests throughout the song and during the final chorus
he is pinned down against the settee while the others continue
to mock him. At the end of the routine, they all laugh.*)

ANNA   Laura! Look at the time! We were supposed to be at that psychology seminar eight minutes ago! Margarite will be waiting for us.

LAURA   Oh no! Come on! Quick, where's my bag? (*Jiri holds it up gingerly between two fingers; she grabs it. Caustically*) Suits you.

(Anna and Laura go off.)

VICTOR   (*Sitting beside Valerie on the settee, looks at her and screws up his face.*) Have you looked in the mirror?

VALERIE   No! I bet I look . . .

VICTOR   Horrific!

VALERIE   (*Bounding to her feet*) Oh well, just wait till you see the transformation.

VICTOR   Have you got a magic wand?

VALERIE   If I had, I'd know whose mouth I'd zip up.

(Valerie goes off.)

PETER   Vic? Have you heard about the new changes in censorship?

VICTOR   Have *you* heard? They've sacked Kudrna, Bartuska and Hendrych from their ministries and Zarnak is out too. The old Moscow puppets are falling like rotten fruit, and rumour has it–it's only rumour, mind you–that Zarnak has taken refuge in the East German Embassy. Officially, he's on holiday.

JIRI   So that's why the apology is in the paper today.

VICTOR   I think so–but never count on Zarnak's giving up.

PETER   (*Picking up his jacket and indicating furiously to Jiri*) Things may be changing, lads, but unless you've forgotten, we said we'd meet Alexus at the café.

JIRI   Right away. Fancy me forgetting that, coming Vic?

VICTOR   No, not yet. I've got to get my notes together and Miss Prague through there is hardly likely to be ready to go out yet.

(Jiri and Peter go off. Victor begins to pad around the room, picking up a few items, including a folder thick with notes. He sits down to thumb through them and Valerie sticks her head comically round the door.)

VALERIE   (*In a dark, sexy voice*) Eez there anyvone at 'ome?

VICTOR   (*Not in the mood for such games*) Face filled in then? Or are you auditioning for a part in a circus?

VALERIE   Oh come off it Vic, you never give me a nice compliment, you're rotten!

VICTOR   That was meant to be a compliment.

VALERIE   (*Sitting down forcibly on the settee*) No it wasn't. You're a rotten beggar when you want to be–you just don't appreciate me.

VICTOR   There's not much to appreciate.

VALERIE   STOP IT! I . . . I don't know when you're kidding.

VICTOR   (*Not knowing when to stop*) Don't sit sideways on, that's cheating . . . I can't see you!

VALERIE Do you want me to be a fat old cow?

VICTOR Is someone out there speaking to me?

VALERIE (*Picks up the cushion and thumps him. She is close to tears.*) I spend all this time – for you – and you just fart about making rude comments. (*Sobs*) It's not fair.

VICTOR (*Trying to put an arm round her*) Ah come on, you know I'm just kidding.

VALERIE No you're not.

VICTOR (*Retreating*) Right, I'm not.

VALERIE You pig.

VICTOR Oh stop it, would you? I was just joking.

VALERIE (*Attacking*) Well I don't like your jokes. You always make jokes at my expense, but you expect *me* to run after you. You just get up and go to your meetings and leave me when it suits you. I'm . . . I'm just a convenience. You tell me I've got marriage on the brain, but it's you who expects me to run at your beck and call. I'm sick of your jokes, of your games, of your laughing at me . . . (*Getting up*) . . . your smart jibes – YOU TREAT ME ROTTEN!

(Valerie stomps out of the room, leaving Victor open-mouthed.)

VICTOR (*Pause*) What did I say now? Women!

(He sits down, uncomfortably, and tries to read some notes. Anna and Laura come bursting in.)

ANNA Hey! Where is everyone? Are Jiri and Peter away? We were too late for the seminar (*Slows down, realising something has gone wrong.*) . . . so we didn't bother going.

LAURA Where's Val?

(Victor doesn't answer. He shrugs his shoulders in apparent indifference.)

Uh huh! Have we had an exchange of words?

(The girls disappear into the next room and quickly reappear in single file. Valerie is in the lead, coat on and carrying her books. They ignore Victor totally. Anna sticks her head back through the curtain.)

ANNA   You *are* a rotten pig!

(Victor gets to his feet, makes after them, stops, sits down again and begins to sing.)

Song: Left Alone

VICTOR   Left alone, time now to think aloud,
Feelings that sense out the truth:
That I'm too proud, too proud to
Say with a smile,
'What was all that shouting about?'
It seemed so important, so real at the time,
Now it's so nothing, the fault must be mine.

If I phone, will she listen?
If I write, will she read?
If I hide near her home and surprise her tomorrow,
Will she walk past, ignore me?
God knows, that's what I need.
If I say it's all my fault,
If I buy her some flowers,
Will she look hard right through me, pretend I'm not there?
She should, yes I know it, but please, I do care.

(The lighting dims. Victor switches on an Anglepoise lamp and begins to write. The door opens and slams. Enter Peter and Jiri.)

VICTOR   Where are the girls? Didn't you see them?

JIRI   Gone home. They decided to come out in support of Valerie in her exploitation by the media classes.

VICTOR   Very funny – are they coming up?

PETER   No. They went *home* and your name is mud.

VICTOR   Good grief, it wasn't as though I meant anything. *(Begins to put on his coat.)*

JIRI   You're not going out at this time of night, are you?

PETER   (*Sarcastically*) So?

VICTOR   Push off – I don't need lip from you two.

SCENE 5   **Outside a deserted café in the streets of Prague. There are chairs on the tables. It is very dark. LAURA, ANNA and MARGARITE are trying to reason with VALERIE.**

LAURA   Look, are you coming home or not?

ANNA   You can't go running back to him now.

MARGARITE   Come on home and have a good sleep. It'll all be so much simpler in the morning.

VALERIE   You three go on ahead. I'll catch up with you later.

ANNA   If you go crawling back to him, I'll, I'll . . . I'll be furious.

VALERIE   OK, OK. Just let me be. I'm a big girl now – you've been telling me that all night. I just need to think things out for myself, that's all.

MARGARITE   Come on then girls, maybe she's right, let's go. It's getting quite cool.

LAURA   Let her be alone.

(Laura, Anna and Margarite go off, leaving Valerie alone.)

Song: Left Alone (Reprise)

VALERIE   Left alone, who wants to be alone?
Walking around in a daze
'Cause I'm too proud, too proud to
Say with a smile,
'What was all that joking about?'
It seemed so important, so mean at the time,
Now it's so meaningless, the fault could be mine.

If he phoned, would I listen?
If he wrote, would I read?
If he hid near my home and surprised me tomorrow,
Would I walk past, ignore him?
God knows what he needs.
If he said it's all his fault,
If he brought me some flowers,
Would I look hard right through him, pretend he's not there?
I should, but I wouldn't, oh please, I do care.

(*Valerie takes down a chair and sits facing the audience.*)

VALERIE   I suppose I've brought all this on myself – chasing him
everywhere as though he were a prize bull. (*Pause*) He's so
kind at times, and then, so very off-hand and arrogant. I
just don't know where I stand. I know there are plenty of
other fish in the sea, but well, look at me, I'm twenty but
I'm behaving like a child. But perhaps I am still a child?
Why do we always try to pretend to be so grown up when
in our heart of hearts we yearn to be free like children
still? It's so confusing. (*Pause*) Who am I? (*Looks up
towards the sky.*) Who is Valerie Kucerova? (*Pause*) Why do
we always ask questions to which we know there is no
answer? Oh God . . . I'm confused. Victor . . . VIC-TOR
. . . why have you abandoned me?

**(Victor has entered unnoticed by Valerie and he replies quite
softly.)**

VICTOR   I haven't abandoned you, honestly.

VALERIE   (*Smarting*) What are you doing here? Go away! I'm not
talking to you.

VICTOR   (*Taking down another seat*) Sorry, I didn't realise.

VALERIE   (*Pointedly*) The café's shut!

VICTOR   Oh! I'll wait.

VALERIE   Well, Mr Big-Time Newsman, who are you going to cut
to ribbons now?

VICTOR   (*Trying to calm her down*) Look, Val, I'm sorry, really very sorry. I didn't mean to be so sarcastic, it's just my way of being 'big' I suppose, but I didn't mean to upset you, honestly. I didn't mean (*drops voice*) to be unkind.

VALERIE   Well you were . . . and . . . and . . . I'm not going to be your doormat. We either work things out or . . . or . . . forget it.

VICTOR   (*Taking a deep breath*) I know I've been taking you for granted . . . . always expecting you to be by my side when I want you . . . but I do get so involved. I do realise you are with me and do miss you when you're not.

VALERIE   Well, you never say so.

VICTOR   I'm saying so now.

VALERIE   Are you sure? (*Victor nods.*) In that case I might just re-establish diplomatic relations . . . provided you put it in the paper.

VICTOR   Put what in the paper?

VALERIE   Notice of our engagement!

VICTOR   (*Springing back*) Engagement?

VALERIE   Engagement!

VICTOR   Wait a minute. There's a hell of a difference between diplomatic relations and marriage.

VALERIE   Oh, I don't know. Both give you licence to take liberties, don't they?

VICTOR   Hey, that's quite smart - can I quote you?

VALERIE   (*Entering into the spirit of the moment*) If you're short of good copy. (*Putting her arm round him*) I'm only joking, but you need the occasional shock to keep you in the world of real people.

VICTOR (*Quite passionately*) But we are in the world of real people . . . and they are making Czechoslovakia shake. Val, things are really moving. Soon, maybe very soon, we could think about settling down, but let's give ourselves time to readjust to all this freedom. Look at Prague – look at us – can't you almost smell the change?

Song: Prague Spring

VICTOR Have you ever seen the quiet dawn
Rise above the square,
Watched the waking morn spread
With silent tender care,

VALERIE Felt the first ray touch your heart,
Suddenly aware
The new day's come, what's passed is gone,
Prague spring is everywhere?

VICTOR, VALERIE Prague spring is all I ever want;
Fresh and friendly, free;
Prague spring will offer every man
The chance of liberty;
Prague spring, let us live
The way we want to be;
Prague spring is ever in my heart;
Prague spring is you and me.

It's so wonderful to be alive on a morning like this,
Wonderful to hold your hand, dare to steal a kiss;
Where else can you dance and waltz
In the middle of the street,
Knowing that it doesn't matter who you chance to meet?

It's so wonderful to be so free on a morning like this,
Wonderful to stay with you, hope to get a kiss;
Where else can we do a twirl in Wenceslas Square?
It's great to do the things you love
Without a worldly care.

VALERIE Do you believe this is really happening?

VICTOR Of course it is, and we are making it happen. Just think of the changes in the last six months.

SCENE 6   The streets of Prague.

(Enter ZARNAK **with** VISCLAV. **They walk across the stage.)**

ZARNAK   This is the trouble with people who think, they think that they know better, especially the young ones, and what is it they really want?

(Zarnak and Visclav go off. STUDENTS **enter from the other side of the stage, including** ANNA, LAURA **and** PETER.**)**

ANNA   All these dismissals inside the Party.

LAURA   I told you Dubcek was a great guy.

PETER   Mind you, we still have a long way to go before all the wrongs of the last twenty years are put right.

(Enter the PEOPLE OF PRAGUE **in wild discussion.)**

MAN 1   A free press . . .

WOMAN 1   A free television . . .

MAN 2   A free nation . . .

WOMAN 2   Czech and Slovak . . .

(Murmerings grow quickly into a chant)

Dubcek!   Dubcek!   We want Dubcek!
Dubcek!   Dubcek!   We want Dubcek!

(Enter PAUL **and** JOHAN. **Paul strides forward angrily.)**

PAUL   Doesn't anyone remember Hungary? This nonsense will have to stop before people really get hurt. *(Pause.)*

JOHAN   Don't be such a pessimist!

PAUL   Huh!

ALL   Dubcek!   Dubcek!   We want Dubcek!

(Into the middle of the company comes LISA.**)**

LISA   *(To Paul)* See. There is hope – and the time is NOW.

Song: Hope (Reprise)

LISA   Time is everlasting, but for us it is today;
      What use is next year, never, the future's made this way.
HALF CAST Keep hope alive, believe again, the truth you cannot hide;
      Have faith in what we can do, history stands fast on our side.
ALL   Take love to guide your footsteps, love of all, who love this land.
      Slovak and Czech – as one rise up – our nation's in your hands.
ALL *(Chorus)* May it be so, may it be so, etc.

End of Act One

ACT TWO

26 June 1968

Inside the Prague Newspaper Office, EMIL, the Editor, is sitting at his desk. From behind a screen by the Editor's desk comes the sound of busy typists. The room is untidy, with filled waste-paper baskets, cups everywhere and plenty of telephones. PAUL is working.

EMIL   KARLA! (*She comes rushing over.*) Retype that, would you, and get the spelling right. TOMAS! TOMAS! Where is my supposedly-efficient assistant? Here man! What do we pay you for? For what time is the editorial meeting scheduled?

(TOMAS comes rushing in, paper in hand.)

TOMAS   For 10.30.

EMIL   Lead stories? What's hot on the wires tonight?

TOMAS   Well, there's . . .

EMIL   You know, this job was easier when we had censorship - I for one had fewer decisions to make.

TOMAS   Emil, you're surely not suggesting that . . .

EMIL   Of course not. Tomas, you have no sense of humour.

(VICTOR bursts in with copies of a fairly bulky document. He throws one across to Paul.)

VICTOR   Read that, and eat your heart out!

EMIL   If that's what I think it is, give it to me.

VICTOR   Yes, Vaculik's 'Two thousand words' is ready for printing:* an open letter from the people, from workers, scientists, doctors, artists, sportsmen, demanding that the new liberties be safeguarded.

PAUL   (*Very angrily*) Of all the stupid things to do! An open letter against the Party! FOLLY! The Russians will jump down your throats for this.

VICTOR   (*Striding up to Paul*) Paul! You're unbelievable. You've forseen Russian intervention at least twice a day since Dubcek became leader. Have you even read the document?

PAUL   I heard rumours that something like this was being prepared, but I didn't think anyone would be so stupid. (*Moving towards Emil*) We can't print this.

VICTOR   We must.

PAUL   This is the end. Who signed it? (*Flicking to end of document*) mmm, huh. Zatopek – that'll cost him his pension. (*Looks up at Victor.*) Oh you stupid blackguard, what did you get involved for?

VICTOR   (*Indignantly*) Why not? I believe in these demands. I'm prepared to stand up for them.

PAUL   You may do so – in Siberia.

VICTOR   Emil, what do you think about these 'Two thousand words'?

EMIL   What do I think? It's *madness*. So you think it means something? Good Lord, man, how many documents has history reduced to the rubbish bin? I thought you were intelligent. This isn't news, it's an act of stupidity. (*Victor tries to butt in.*)

* See page 71 for extracts from this document.

PAUL Before you start, just ask yourself: what real weight do professors, clergymen, students and reporters have? Will Workers' Councils be able to stop the Moscow moguls from using this as key evidence that Czechoslovakia is being over-run by subversives?

EMIL Can't you see that the consequences of this could be an end to all our gains and lead us right back to the Stalin era? The Warsaw Pact manoeuvres are due to start *here* in a few weeks, and what an excuse this could be for the troops to stay.

VICTOR But we have broken away from the past. We are trying to consolidate Czechoslovakia's future.

PAUL It's worse than folly. Do we have to go through the pains of Budapest yet again? Has everyone forgotten '56? Oh, Krushchev may have gone, but don't delude yourself. Brezhnev is still the master . . . the game is still 'possession' and they won't let us go.

EMIL (*Trying to be kinder*) All this talk: 'a new fresh hope', a 'change in the economy', an 'Action Programme', these are empty phrases - they don't mean anything.

PAUL Do you think the Party will surrender everything? Dubcek has already gone too far too fast, and time is not on his side, or your side, or Czechoslovakia's side.

EMIL That's so. You may be well-intentioned but how far do good intentions get you? One thing is certain: we are not publishing it!

Song: Two Thousand Words

EMIL, PAUL What is this madness, do you think that these are more than words?
How many documents has history reduced to the absurd?
I thought you were intelligent, the cream of studenthood;
You bring me this as though it's news - I'd burn it if I could.
Before you start, just stop and think, you really ought to know,
What use are all these signatures before an iron foe?

Will professors and clergymen, reporters or students,
Or all the Workers' Councils be able to prevent
The kind of righteous anger which delights our Moscow friends
And gives them ample reason to strike and make amends?
You seem to think me weak and scared because I will not print
The schemes and aims of well-intentioned fools who cannot
    think,
But let me try to make you see, the consequence of this could be
The end of all our gains and even lead backwards;
The army games are due to start, by chance they're coming
    here.
Just one false move and we could all be out of work next year.

What is this rashness, it's the one thing that they won't have
    here.
How many innocents have died in *vain* to make that clear?
Have you forgotten '56, things haven't changed that much?
Our Moscow masters know the score, they'll keep us in their
    clutch,
And all this talk of 'real fresh hope', a 'new economy',
Believe you me is just a sham, we dance the cossack way.
What use's an 'Action Programme' and 'Public Confidence'?
Empty phrases that really don't mean sense.
Above all else the greatest sin is challenging their power;
A National Front, free speech, you'll see it all turn sour.
They'll never bend the Party line, nor let their iron grip
    decline;
I tell you now this whole thing's rushed, please take this tip:
Clear your head of wild romance, be practical, don't take a
    chance.
Are you the bright young man I thought – or blind to fate?
I promise you, time's running out, I know you all mean well,
But good intentions, don't you see, will pave the road to hell.

VICTOR *(Who has consistently refused to be impressed or moved by this argument)* But Emil, we must carry it. It's what the people want. The other papers will, that's for sure.

EMIL *(Getting as angry as Victor)* Let them!

PAUL No one should carry it.

VICTOR They are going to – we owe it to our readers to publish it in full. We can't hide it from them.

EMIL   (*Snapping his fingers*) No, that we cannot, but *we* will merely mention it. I'm not publishing the whole document. *We* have a duty to Czechoslovakia too, and the best thing we can do is to play down this 'over-enthusiasm'.

VICTOR   But . . .

EMIL   No buts! Paul, write a short front-page acknowledgement without any political comment. No detail.

PAUL   Right.

VICTOR   That's censorship.

EMIL   It's self-control – and that, my boy, is what you, and your comrades, need.

SCENE 2   The Newspaper Office. JOHAN is on the telephone. He is alone. A kettle sits on the floor and evidence of a hard night's work lies around.

JOHAN   You're sure? Absolutely sure? I'll read it back to you. Correct me if anything is out of context. You've been on holiday in East Germany and you've just returned home. Right? Right! The East Germans diverted you away from the main roads because of the massive military build up . . . said there were to be more manoeuvres . . . right? No, no, I must be honest, we have no details at all about any further manoeuvres . . . I thought they were to be finished too. Yes, yes, of course you are worried. Tanks, you say, and they are definitely facing towards our side of the border? OK, OK . . . I'll phone the Ministry and see if I can raise any answers. Thank you very much . . . OK . . . goodbye. (*Scribbles down a few notes.*) Hell, that's very strange. Vic? Paul?

(PAUL comes in first, in shirt sleeves and looking tired. He is followed by VICTOR.)

PAUL   It's too late for the morning edition, no matter what it is. What is it?

JOHAN   Maybe nothing–maybe we should get hold of Emil.

PAUL   For nothing? What is it?

VICTOR   What's wrong?

JOHAN   Maybe nothing–maybe war!

VICTOR   War?

JOHAN   I have had three phone calls in the last half hour: two from the border, one from a tourist, and all say that the East Germans are lined up to pounce. Tanks, troops, the *lot*.

VICTOR   Calm yourself, man, it can't be. The army manoeuvres are officially over–even most of the Russkis have gone home now.

PAUL   How far home? *(He turns to Johan.)* Get Emil.

(He picks up another telephone and dials.)

VICTOR   Who are you calling?

PAUL   The Praesidium Office–I want an official reply.

VICTOR   Will you get one?

PAUL   I bloody hope so.

JOHAN   Emil, could you come to the office immediately, please? We have reason to believe that we are about to be invaded. No sir, I have *not* been drinking.

(Paul takes over, exchanging phones with Johan.)

PAUL   Emil, this is Paul. We're very serious. *(Pause)* Would I joke? Thank you. *(Puts down phone.)*

JOHAN   Get as many of the typists as have telephones out of their beds. There must be an index somewhere.

PAUL   The wireless–we may get a news flash. In fact, I'll phone Stanislaw at the radio news desk. They may have a report.

(The three of them are by now scurrying about in a mild panic. Victor is still standing holding onto the phone for Paul when a voice answers at the other end.)

VICTOR   I'm through . . . oh . . . er . . . is that the Praesidium Office? Yes, well, here's Paul.

PAUL   Pardon my young friend. He has just had a shock. This is the news office, can you confirm or deny a report that the East Germans and the Russians are about to invade us? When? NOW, man, NOW. (*Pause*) Nothing! (*Quietening down slightly*) No reports at all? Is the army alerted? No! (*He puts down the phone.*) They say 'no'.

JOHAN   I'm through to Stan at the radio desk.

PAUL   Stan, have you any reports from the border of military activity . . . yes? Yes, so have we. The Praesidium claims to have heard nothing . . . the line to the border is dead! What? Why? That's ridiculous . . . *why?* Someone in top management knows something . . . try to get your technicians out as fast as you can! (*Puts down the phone.*) It must be true . . . some high-ranking Party official has given orders that the engineers switch off radio transmitters tonight.

VICTOR   What? Why?

PAUL   Because, if the Russians are coming, they don't want any news broadcast.

(The phone rings violently; Johan leaps on it.)

JOHAN   Yes? Yes. (*Covering the phone*) It's the Bratislava Office. Oh God (*pause*) you're certain? (*Looking at his watch*) God help you brother . . . be careful. (*Putting down the phone*) Soviet troops moved into Bratislava just before midnight tonight.

VICTOR   Any fighting?

JOHAN   I never asked, he never said. But what do you think? Against Russia?

PAUL   (*Turning to pick up his jacket*) Goodnight, Prague.

SCENE 3   21 August 1968

> *Wenceslas Square in the centre of Prague. Soviet tanks in obvious evidence. The people in the streets are angry and vociferous. One tank is in the centre of the stage, manned by a RUSSIAN GUNNER.*

WOMAN 1   What are you doing here? Get that monster out of my city.

WOMAN 2   Shame on you – we are peace-loving people – go home.

> *(The gathering crowd grows ever more menacing.)*

MAN 1   Get going, Russki, we want to be Czech and Slovak, not Russian.

MAN 2   *(Baring his chest to the tank gun)* Come on then, blow Czech socialism away.

RUSSIAN GUNNER   *(Looking perplexed)* But we have been sent to save you, comrade, from subversion.

WOMEN   Where is this subversion? You see only Czechs. Czechs who wish to be Czechs. Show me evidence of disruption in Prague, come on, show me!

RUSSIAN GUNNER   *(Embarrassed)* We have orders!

MAN 1   Stuff your orders – give us the right to be ourselves. We want Dubcek; he is a good leader.

CROWD   Yes, we want Dubcek *(Begin to chant.)*

> Dubcek!   Dubcek!   We want Dubcek.
> Dubcek!   Dubcek!   We want Dubcek.
> Go home!   Go home!   Go home Russki.
> Go home!   Go home!   Go home Russki.

Song: Go Home Russki

CROWD   You're not wanted here, carrions of fear, can't you sense our
    disgust?
    To your offer of tanks, Dubcek answered 'No thanks',
    That even *you* could have sussed.

Where are the traitors, or Communist baiters?
It's plain to see they do not exist.
Your mission's a lie, you cannot deny, we greet you here with
    raised fist.

So, Go home Russki – back to the Volga;
       Go home Russki – put away your revolver;
       Go home Russki – take your tanks back;
       Go home and stay there – that's all we ask.

Get out of our square, how can you dare pretend that we are
    your friends?
Your guns are a threat, your leaders are set to use us for their
    own ends.
Is your confidence such that you have to touch every state with
    cold fear?
Is the point of a gun the way that it's done?
You're friendless in Prague, that's clear.

So, Go home Russki, etc.

Get out of our city, have you no pity for people who wish to be
    free?
Get out of our lives, our children, our wives want it that way,
    can't you see?
Get back to the Steppes, you iron clad reps of a system we no
    longer want;
Can't you feel our real hate for your miserable State, its truth;
    that's what we taunt.

So, Go home Russki, etc.

(VICTOR, JIRI, JAN **and the other students move to front of stage
and begin to get themselves organised. One of their number is**
MARK.)

VICTOR   OK. Peter, you get the transmitter from the faculty to the
flat. Jiri, try to get some auxiliary back-up systems from
the barracks, your brother should be able to help. Jan, we
must get those leaflets printed and distributed and keep
in touch with the TV.

MARK   What about me, Vic? I want to do something to help.

VICTOR   If Zarnak gets you, you won't be able to deny everything
this time.

MARK   (*Aware of his past denial*) Look, Vic, I know that . . .

VICTOR   Forget it. We need every willing hand *now*. Come on.

(**They go off, leaving a fair number of the milling mob still protesting. Two RUSSIAN SOLDIERS appear and move towards an OLD WOMAN carrying bread.**)

SOLDIER 1   Hey, let's get some bread, I'm starving.

SOLDIER 2   Lady, lady, how much is the bread?

BREADWOMAN   What bread?

SOLDIER 1   That bread.

BREADWOMAN   Oh, it's not for sale.

SOLDIER 2   *What*! That's ridiculous.

BREADWOMAN   It's all ordered.

SOLDIER 1   I . . . I don't believe you.

BREADWOMAN   Too bad, sonny. It's not for sale to *you* let me tell you. If I had a lorry-load of bread, a bakery full of bread, I wouldn't give you a crumb, not a stale crumb.

(**She storms off. LISA comes across the stage, only to be accosted by the same two.**)

SOLDIER 1   Excuse me, Madam, but . . . er . . . would you like some company?

SOLDIER 2   Or two companies? (*They laugh and deliberately obstruct her.*)

LISA   (*In outraged anger*) Is it not enough that you force your attentions on all of Czechoslovakia, or is the rape of an innocent nation only the prelude to worse?

SOLDIER 2   What do you mean? We have money. (*He takes some notes out of his pockets. Lisa angrily knocks it away.*)

LISA   Don't you understand? Get lost . . . get out . . . leave us *now*!

(**They are rudely interrupted by the PRIEST, who indignantly puts himself between the troops and Lisa.**)

PRIEST What is the meaning of this? How dare you accost this young lady? (*Turning to her*) Are you all right, my dear?

LISA (*Regaining her poise*) Yes thank you, Father.

SOLDIERS (*Perplexed*) But we . . .

PRIEST Come along with me, my dear – the shock must have upset you.

LISA Why yes, Father, thank you.

(They go off, leaving the two Russian soldiers.)

SCENE 4 **Night. A wall in the city. The girls are trying to manoeuvre a rather heavy ladder up the side wall in the darkness.**

ANNA Over a bit, over a bit.

VALERIE Ssh! We must be careful.

MARGARITE This is silly – I must be off my head.

LAURA Who's going up?

MARGARITE Not me.

ANNA OK, me again, but hold that ladder steady.

VALERIE (*Whispering*) OK?

LAURA Come on, we can't hang around for too long.

ANNA I feel like a commando.

LAURA Well, you're not getting one, so hurry up.

VALERIE What? What was that about commandos?

MARGARITE (*Frightened*) Oh no! Where? Where?

LAURA Quiet, don't move, someone's coming.

(They freeze, afraid to look. The approaching figure turns out to be LISA.)

LISA What's this – competition?

ANNA Ssh!

VALERIE Ssh!

LISA (*Loud whisper*) What are you doing?

LAURA Getting as many street signs as we can to confuse the Russkis.

LISA Oh, can they read them, these Russians?

VALERIE Eh . . . not if they're not there, they can't.

ANNA Stop bickering and hold the ladder steady.

MARGARITE Ssh, I think someone else is coming.

LAURA Get on with it.

VALERIE She's right - run!

ANNA What!

(**They don't know where to run, so they end up in a rather static position when two** POLICE OFFICERS **with torches arrive.**)

PC 1 All right . . . stay where you are . . . don't move (*He shines his torch on their faces.*) Well, well, well, and what piece of nonsense is this?

ANNA It's not nonsense, it's a protest, didn't you know?

LAURA Or are you happy to live in an occupied city? Glad to see your Russian friends?

PC 2 Cut out the cheek. What are you doing? Removing street signs? What a major effect this is going to have! You're just playing childish games.

ANNA At least we're not supporting *them*.

PC 1 I'm not going to waste my time with you - you can explain it all to the desk sergeant at the Police Station.

LISA   (*Who has been hidden slightly at the back*) Excuse me – Andrei – isn't it? You know I haven't seen you since you were married. How are you? Your wife? I see her sometimes in the department store – haberdashery – you know. Andrei, I sometimes get this wicked desire to ask her how you are getting on. She seems such a nice girl.

PC 1   Ehm! Yes, yes, she is. Well, ehm, look, you lot had better be very careful. There are troops in the streets, and some others less considerate than us – so be careful.

(The policemen retreat.)

LAURA   Oh Lisa, you were brilliant, I thought we were done for.

LISA   Forget it, he knows when to leave matters as they are.

ANNA   Keep hold of the ladder. *(She has still to prise off the street sign.)*

VALERIE   Hurry up, let's get this job finished.

MARGARITE   (*Clinging to the ladder*) I wish I'd stayed at home.

LAURA   (*Caustically*) I wish you'd stayed at home too.

   (They are on the point of bickering when Anna screams in delight.)

ANNA   (*Proudly displaying the sign*) Got it!

VALERIE   (*With relief*) Good.

(Laura makes to move off with the ladder before Anna has descended, causing considerable panic.)

ANNA   Hold on! **(She scurries down.)**

ANNA   Oh hurry up, please.

VALERIE   Come on, and don't forget the ladder.

(Lisa shakes her head and laughs as they all go off in considerable disarray.)

SCENE 5   **21-28 August 1968**

The stage is split in two: to the left is the Russian High
Command, with ZARNAK close at hand; to the right the boys'
room at the university transformed into a makeshift studio. In
the Russian section a COMMANDER is giving dictation to a
MAJOR.

RUSSIAN   (*Clipboard in hand*) Send this message to Moscow: 'Invasion
COMMANDER   a complete success. Bratislava taken at midnight. Prague
fell at 3.30 a.m. The Praesidium and Dubcek are under
arrest.'

ZARNAK   The radio has broadcast a message announcing that the
five Warsaw Pact armies participated in the invasion, and
it asks that the people stay calm.

RUSSIAN   (*With a sarcastic smile*) Quite wise, but watch these
COMMANDER   reactionaries, do not trust them. Mind you (*an
afterthought*) I did not expect the Czechs to match the
Hungarians in spirit. (*To his major*) Did you?

RUSSIAN MAJOR   No sir.

ZARNAK   (*Almost proudly*) But the people are not very co-operative,
are they?

RUSSIAN   No, they are not! And that must be stopped – a measure
COMMANDER   of respect for law and order is needed right now.

ZARNAK   You mean fear?

RUSSIAN   We have the numbers, we must use them profitably.
COMMANDER

(Action switches to the boys' room, where a transmitter
dominates the tables with telephones.)

JIRI   We've got four underground stations and the A1
transmitter. We can broadcast to the nation, and to the
world. The Russians won't know what has hit them.

PETER   Here's hoping. The people are at least making their
feelings evident.

JAN   I've seen them sitting in front of tanks.

VICTOR   Yes, and I've heard that farmers are refusing point-blank to sell either grain or potatoes to the invaders, and shopkeepers are putting up signs which say: 'No Russians served here.'

PETER   They say that some Russian troops are crying with hunger. (*They laugh.*) And boy, are they *stupid*! You've heard that they are confiscating all transistor radios?

JIRI   Yes?

PETER   So, if they see anyone holding a square object to their ears, they confiscate it? Anna's already had two cornflake packets and a lump of coal confiscated! Thick!

(**Enter** VALERIE, **with** ANNA, MARGARET **and** LAURA, **carrying a selection of street signs.**)

JIRI   What in heaven's name . . . ?

ANNA   Well, they won't be able to move around Prague and make selected arrests if they don't know where they are.

VICTOR   Let's see.

(**They proudly display a huge sign which says 'Wenceslas Square'. Victor gives Valerie a hug.**)

Well done, team, mind you, they might be able to guess where Wenceslas Square is.

MARGARITE   How about these?

LAURA   Or these?

(**Laughter all round.**)

PETER   We're on our way – one week of starvation and propaganda and these troops won't know whether they are coming or going.

(**The action switches to the Russian High Command. The Commander is on the telephone alone.**)

RUSSIAN COMMANDER   In twenty-four hours we have reached a position of stalemate . . . we are in control . . . of nothing. I agree we do not want violence . . . or any martyrs, but . . . these disappearing street signs . . . these stupid protests must stop (*Bangs his fist.*) But most of all the illegal radios *must* be silenced. Get Moscow on the line. I want the latest radio detectors and jammers . . . HERE . . . NOW . . . IMMEDIATELY.

(Action switches to boys' room: Victor on the radio.)

VICTOR   This is Radio Free Prague . . . we thank all our listeners for their composure, and for the quiet, reassuring way they are showing the invading forces exactly how they feel. The Russian Commander in Prague is most distressed about our radio broadcasts, and we have been reliably informed that in one hour a train will cross the border carrying radio-jamming and detection equipment. People of Czechoslovakia, we would be well served if this train did not reach Prague.

(Switch to the Russian High Command.)

RUSSIAN COMMANDER   (*On phone*) Well? Well? Where is the equipment? Look! It left Moscow two days ago. Where is it! What? What do you mean 'held up'? Where? Why? (*Pause*) Well arrest the stationmaster . . . push through the papers . . . AND GET ME THAT EQUIPMENT!

(Switch to the boys' room.)

VICTOR   (*On phone*) Great, great, well done, man. Yes, we will broadcast the news. The people will remember. (*Puts down the phone.*) Guess what, the Russians have got the train moving, but unfortunately the overhead electricity supply has failed and it is stuck on the line. (*Cheers.*)

JAN   (*Pensively*) How long for?

PETER   Cheer up, Jan, we must look on the bright side.

(Switch to the Russian High Command.)

RUSSIAN COMMANDER So? So? Is that supposed to be an excuse? Would you like a posting to the Chinese border? Get a secondary supply system . . . man the power station . . . use a steam train . . . use your brain. I warn you, if I have to leave Prague to get this equipment, heads will roll.

(Switch to the boys' room.)

VICTOR (*Into microphone*) With regard to the radio equipment which our Russian invaders need to silence us. I am proud to announce that it is now sitting in a certain countryside siding. Our sincerest thanks to the brave drivers and signalmen who guided it there. Our thanks too, to the other engine drivers who have parked their engines in front of the train so that it is now well and truly stuck. Let the world now measure the determination of the Czech and Slovak people to remain free from Russian domination.

(Switch to the Russian High Command.)

RUSSIAN COMMANDER It's what? (*Pause*) Where? (*Pause*) What . . . do . . . you . . . mean . . . you don't *exactly* know? You don't KNOW! Find that train. You can't simply lose a train- not even you- find it, find it. I want that machine NOW.

(Switch to the boys' room.)

PETER (*On phone*) What? Damn! Are you sure? Oh no, it's only a question of time now. Yes, thanks.

VICTOR What is it?

ANNA Bad news?

PETER They've picked up the jamming equipment by helicopter; it's on its way to Prague. We may only have one hour's transmission time left before they jam us forever.

Song: Calling the Free World

ALL   Calling the free world from Radio Prague:
The tanks have taken over from our trams;
They roam the streets like packs of dogs,
Protecting us from freedom's wrongs,
And dangerous democracy;
Calling the free world, can you hear me?

Listen to us now, it's Radio Prague:
Our leaders have been taken into care,
And Russian iron clanks ominous threats,
Deaf to protests, tears or wrath;
We must be saved, they say.
Calling the free world, can you act today?

If anyone's out there, it's Radio Prague:
This city doesn't want to lose its soul;
All we ask is the right to be ourselves,
Not strip our minds, our hearts, our home;
We must conform, they say.
Calling the free world, can't you keep them at bay?

Hear us while you can, it's Radio Prague:
So much has happened to us overnight;
The promised dawn of Dubcek's new reforms
Has faded into darker backward ways;
Change is not a word that Moscow will bear.
Calling the free world, do you really care?

Goodbye free world from Radio Prague:
Though your cameras have clicked and newsreel rolled,
Our story doesn't seem to move your powers.
You won't risk a fight 'cause it could be war,
So freedom falls.

Calling the free world,
Calling the free world,
Do you hear our calls?

(*Repeat the last three lines.*)

SCENE 6 January 1969

> Prague: troops are still in evidence. PAUL is seated at the café having a drink.
>
> (VICTOR enters and crosses quickly to his side.)

VICTOR Paul, have you seen Johan?

PAUL No, isn't he at the office?

VICTOR (*In considerable distress*) NO! Look at this – I've been fired.

PAUL (*Without looking up*) I know, I advised it.

VICTOR What! (*Taken aback*) Why?

PAUL (*As kindly as he can*) So that you will get the message: you will not fit into this 'new' Czechoslovakia: all these trendy ideas of yours, and of those like you, have led to this, to this occupation.

VICTOR (*Rising*) You old fool, are you just going to accept this?

PAUL Yes, yes, I am. There is no other way, my boy – no other way without invoking the end of the world.

VICTOR You *are* a fool and, like so many others around, a coward. I'm not going to waste my time with you – goodbye.

> (Victor goes off.)

PAUL (*Hurt*) A fool? *Me* – a fool?

The Fool's Song

PAUL Sometimes it pays to be the fool
When all around are wise,
Act out the role they cast you in,
Keep free from crippling ties,
Pretend to have forgotten
How the world demands each move,
Then emerge as if from thin air
In an unexpected groove;
For wisdom is the fool's plaything,
He keeps it by his side:

A secret weapon no one sees,
So it doesn't have to hide.
A quiet hint, a subtle phrase,
A chance word out of place,
And watch the wise man look again,
A blush upon his face.

They think I sit here, drinking most times,
Was good in days long past,
A cynic voice that time rusted up,
But they're not in my class.
Oh sure, I once wrote just what I thought,
Found questions that struck deep,
But I survived by soon finding out
When *not* to give a cheep.

I could have told them months ago
That it would end this way,
But they'd have just laughed in my face,
Spoke condescendingly.
They're young – they know – or so they think,
But they've played out their cards;
And now that Dubcek's pack is aced
They've nothing but placards.

Remember this harsh lesson well:
Don't wear an open heart;
Let prudence guard your every word,
And truth remain apart;
Play down your strength of character,
For this may suit your needs,
That way you win their confidence
And so the fool succeeds.

**(He gulps down his coffee and goes. Almost immediately, JAN,
JIRI and PETER come wandering on. They sit down.)**

PETER I'm sick of all this: sick of no one doing anything, sick of
the silence, the cowardly silence.

JAN It's *our* silence, it's our cowardice. If anyone has to make
a move, it's us. We can't blame others: the Germans, the
Americans, the British. Would you risk World War III to
save Czechoslovakia?

JIRI   Yes, yes, I would.

JAN   Then you don't understand. We are not as important as
that. The world accepts us as part of the balance of
natural power: we are the Russians' plaything – and we can
get spanked for being bad boys.

(**Enter** MARK **in a state of alarm.**)

MARK   Where's Victor?

PETER   What's up?

MARK   Zarnak. *(They all react.)* Zarnak, that's what's up. He and
his goons are back on the streets. They bundled me into a
car about an hour ago and wanted to know all about
Victor and his 'Counter-revolutionary activities'.

JIRI   *(Grabs Mark.)* What did you tell him, you little yelp?

MARK   Nothing! Nothing! I gave them a false address, but it
won't take them long to find out.

JAN   This is where it comes home to roost. We are dead
politically, and we are doing nothing about it – NOTHING.
Four months ago we were kidding ourselves that stealing
road signs and delaying a train was an act of aggression,
but where has peaceful protest led us? Nowhere!

(**Victor and** VALERIE **enter with** LAURA, ANNA **and**
MARGARITE. **Depression stalks them. Mark moves to catch**
Victor first.)

MARK   Vic, Zarnak – he's on the streets. He's looking for you.

VALERIE   Oh no!

VICTOR   That's all I need.

JAN   Vic, everyone, sit down. *(They do so, heavy-heartedly.)* We
have to do something, Vic. Something practical,
something physical, something that will cry out amidst
this silence and scream 'STOP'!

PETER   We haven't got the resources.

JIRI   We could surely get some guns–some grenades–blow up the Soviet Embassy?

ANNA   You wouldn't get near it.

VICTOR   And what would happen? We'd just heap the coals of hell on the heads of innocent people, or be killed ourselves . . .

JAN   And would that be so bad?

MARGARITE   Don't talk like that.

JAN   What we need is massive publicity–some protest which will catch the imagination of all Czechs, of the world.

LAURA   A suicide? Like the Buddhists in Vietnam?

(*Victor and Jan look at each other.*)

VICTOR   That's what we were saying last night.

ANNA   Like a kamikaze pilot?

PETER   Same impact–different method.

JAN   Yes, that's what we agreed last night–the human protest! We must go ahead, now. Today.

MARGARITE   It's a sin to take your own life . . .

JAN   (*Rasps*) It is a sin to take the life of a nation.

PETER   Sin is a personal pain. It is not the same thing inside everyone. If a starving man steals a crust of bread to live, is that a sin?

VICTOR   If a man gives up his life for his country, is that a sin?

MARGARITE   Yes.

OTHERS   No.

MARK   But would you go through with it?

VICTOR   Yes.

JIRI   Yes.

JAN   Yes.

VALERIE   I would too if . . . (*She almost says 'Vic'.*)

PETER   Then we draw lots. Whoever picks number one does it - goes first - gives their life for Czechoslovakia. Give me a pen.

(He writes down a few numbers on a piece of paper.)

PETER   Are you in, Mark?

(*He shakes his head.*)

Margarite?

(*She also shakes her head.*)

MARGARITE   You're just being silly.

VICTOR   We'll see.

PETER   That's seven numbers. Number one goes first, and then we follow in order, unless they give way, or Czechoslovakia rises.

(Slowly they take numbers. They all hold their pieces of paper close to themselves.)

JIRI   Well? I've drawn number four - who has number one?

(Peter looks, breathes out, and shakes his head.)

JAN   (*Standing up and moving forward.*) I have . . . I really have . . . and . . . I will.

VICTOR   Wait Jan, if only . . .

JAN   NO! No 'waits'. Procrastination is the first step backwards. I want to think. I'll write a message - but no 'waits'.

MARGARITE   He won't do it. You lot are just kidding.

PETER   Are we?

Song: In Childhood Fantasy

JAN In childhood fantasy, I walked unarmed in Daniel's den;
Fear was no emotion
Which could stop my fervour then;
Crusades were what I lived for,
Riding high and wild;
No armour plate can crush the zest
Which then invades a child.

I fought for God and glory
'Gainst foes without a face,
Knew nothing of the politics which now divide our race,
Cared more for football passion
Ice hockey and TV,
Heard tales of Tomas Masaryk
And wished that he was me.

If only I could dream again,
Ignore reality,
See no tanks or foreign troops,
Believe that I was free;
Fill the square with happy crowds,
Bring back Dubcek's kind,
But dreaming does not alter time:
It just deceives the mind.

What can I offer for this land? My life? Who's heard of Jan?
And if I do, will everyone dub me a madman?
Someone, somewhere must raise his voice,
Stand up and act right now;
Must it be me? Why not? Why not?
I freely took that vow.

Will anyone remember me? Will death release my soul?
Will Czech and Slovak take a stance, make freedom's rights
   their goal?
My life is not so great a gift
But it's all that I have to give,
And if alternatives mean chains,
What reason's there to live?

In childhood fantasy I walked
Unarmed in Daniel's den;
Today I take my final steps . . . Amen

(Voice over Tannoy.)

On 16 January 1969, Jan Palach, a student at the Charles University of Prague, set himself alight in protest against the Russian invasion. He left behind this note:

Because our nations are on the brink of despair
We have decided to express our protest
And to wake up the people of this land.
Our group is composed of volunteers
Who are willing to burn themselves
For our cause.
It was my honour to draw the lot number one
And thus I acquired the privilege of writing the
First letter
And starting as the first torch.
Our demands are:
(1) immediate elimination of censorship
(2) prohibition of the distribution of Zpravy.
If our demands are not fulfilled within five days,
By 21 January 1969,
And if the people do not support us sufficiently,
Through a strike of indefinite duration,
More torches will burn.
Remember August.
In international politics a place was made for
Czechoslovakia.
Let us use it.

Jan died three days later from his terrible burns. His funeral became an expression of national mourning.

SCENE 7 (The stage is set with a single coffin on a catafalque covered in flowers. The STUDENTS and the PEOPLE OF PRAGUE file past the coffin. Some carry single flowers and drop them on the coffin. Some stop and kneel for a moment. Two of the students carry in the Czechoslovak flag and roughly drape the coffin. The words of the Latin requiem are sung.)

Requiem aeternam dona eis Domine:
et lux perpetua luceat eis.

Te decet hymnus, Deus in Sion:
et tibi redetur votum in Jerusalem;
Exaudi orationem meam,
ad te omnis caro veniet.
Kyrie eleison, Christe eleison,
Kyrie eleison. Amen.

Jan's Song

ALL   When the day is done, and our fight is won or lost,
No more could any man do than you did to your cost.
We will never forget, don't you have a regret it was you
Who stood up to say:
'We don't want it this way.'

Now you've won back some pride,
Though the Soviet tide surges on.
The world stands aghast at the way
That you passed your life on.
Hold high your head,
Though your body is dead,
Our hearts are with you – live on Jan.

Though you're first in the draw, did you think it a raw deal
As you poised to protest? Was there fear in your breast?
I never thought that you really would do such a thing.
But you stood as a light
'Gainst the Russian might.

Now you've won back some pride, etc.

When the last autumn leaf falls free in relief, you remain;
Though the Party denies, you're alive in our eyes.
In giving your life to highlight our strife against force,
You stood out alone – Russki go home!

Now you've won back some pride, etc.

(The crowd begins to disperse, leaving VICTOR **and** VALERIE.
They are joined by PAUL **and** JOHAN.)

JOHAN   Vic, you must get out of the country, today.

VICTOR Today? Why so soon? I know Zarnak is after me, but why today?

PAUL Listen, for once in your life, listen.

VICTOR From you I need no advice.

JOHAN Zarnak has a warrant out for your arrest, for anti-State activities, but it will never come to trial. People everywhere are losing their jobs – you've lost yours – and he wants to make an example to youth, through you. He fears you might be the next to commit suicide. He wants *you* before you become a public martyr.

VICTOR What nonsense! Anyway, where could I go?

JOHAN I'll take you to the border. I have some contacts – it won't be difficult.

VICTOR But what about my life here?

PAUL IT'S FINISHED, surely you must realize that?

VICTOR What do you think, Val?

VALERIE (*Surprised*) Oh Vic, I don't know. Go, go, there's no future for you here.

VICTOR (*Pause, then quickly*) OK, we'll go, there *is* no choice?

VALERIE We'll?

VICTOR You're coming too, aren't you?

VALERIE Am I? Do you expect me to go off into exile with you?

VICTOR Yes . . . Look Val . . .

PAUL (*Pushing Valerie towards him*) Go, go now, both of you. Take care, there is still much to be done but it cannot be done here. Take this chance, your friends will see you safe, but *go,* don't linger, and don't come back.

(**Victor moves away. Valerie hugs Johan and Paul and runs after him.**)

THE MAKING OF THE PLAY

Czechmate was written as a musical in a partnership between Bill
Kinross, our head of music at Alva Academy, and myself. Over the
previous five years, we had produced such classics as *Oh What a Lovely
War, West Side Story* and *Paint Your Wagon*. This meant that we had a
solid body of quite experienced actors and actresses, but we were all
itching to do something which would not only be more interesting but
would also challenge us. We also needed to find a topic that would
inspire us in our writing.

Both Bill and I had been students in 1968 when the invasion of
Czechoslovakia took place. At the time, we had identified with our
fellow students in Czechoslovakia; now we were teaching about it as part
of our history lessons. The idea for *Czechmate* took root. First we wrote
some songs, such as 'Calling the Free World' and 'Jan's Song', and tried
them out on the blackboard to get pupils' reactions. They were
enthusiastic – indeed, very enthusiastic – and so we continued until both
the story and the fourteen songs had been written.

The play took months to rehearse and the going wasn't always easy.
Because we were doing a play with such a serious theme, it was
sometimes difficult to keep our spirits up, especially with an ending that
was so depressing. But we managed. On a few occasions when we were
rehearsing the scene where the students pick numbers to see who is to
commit suicide, one or two jokers would say: 'Ooh I've got number one'
just at the most dramatic moment. We soon put a stop to that when Bill
told them that the next person who thought they had drawn number one
had to sing Jan's long and difficult song on his own in front of the whole
cast. That quickly left poor Jan with number one.

The opening night was hair-raising for all of us. Everyone had put so
much into the production – not just the acting and the singing but the
props as well. You try building a full-size Russian tank which can be put
up and taken down in ninety seconds! Perhaps the most important
member of the audience on the first night was a Czech who had seen the
Russian invasion of Prague as a fifteen-year-old boy. He was obviously
moved by the performance and described it as 'spookily real'. That was
the best compliment of all.

Czechmate went on tour all over Scotland. We finally ended a two year
marathon by showing it at the Edinburgh Festival in 1981. We gave ten
performances in a converted church beneath the castle walls. We were
exhausted but none of us would ever be the same again.

Gerry Docherty

FOLLOW-UP ACTIVITIES

Casting the play

Before the play can be put on stage the director has to cast the parts. He needs to find actors who look right, sound right and will be able to understand how the character they are chosen to play feels. Also, in a musical like *Czechmate*, it is important for the actor to be able to sing the songs required of that character. A director cannot have a fixed idea of how the part will be interpreted because each actor will bring his or her individual interpretation to the part. However, it is still essential that the director has a clear idea of the kind of actor he is looking for.

For example, the first director of *Czechmate* wrote notes on each of the characters before he began to cast the play. This is what he wrote about Victor:

Victor: a student of about twenty years old, active, if not at times almost breathless, bursting with energy.

Tends to be so very wrapped up in his own involvement in the exciting changes taking place in Czechoslovakia that he ignores Valerie or takes her for granted.

Has to be able to inject powerful energy and yet be very humble and tender at one stage when Valerie calls his bluff over their relationship.

Must be physically fit and capable of subtle movement.

Imagine you are the director of a production of *Czechmate*. Write casting notes on the following characters:

Zarnak	Russian Commander
Anna	Jan
Peter	Valerie

Your notes should show what you think the character is like; what he or she looks like; what sort of voice or accent he or she will have.

It is sometimes helpful to think of examples of the kind of person you mean from among people or actors you already know. They could be people in your school or actors you have seen on television.

Designing the Play

In its first school production *Czechmate* was performed on a very traditional stage, but the stage was extended to make the audience feel part of the play. The set looked like this:

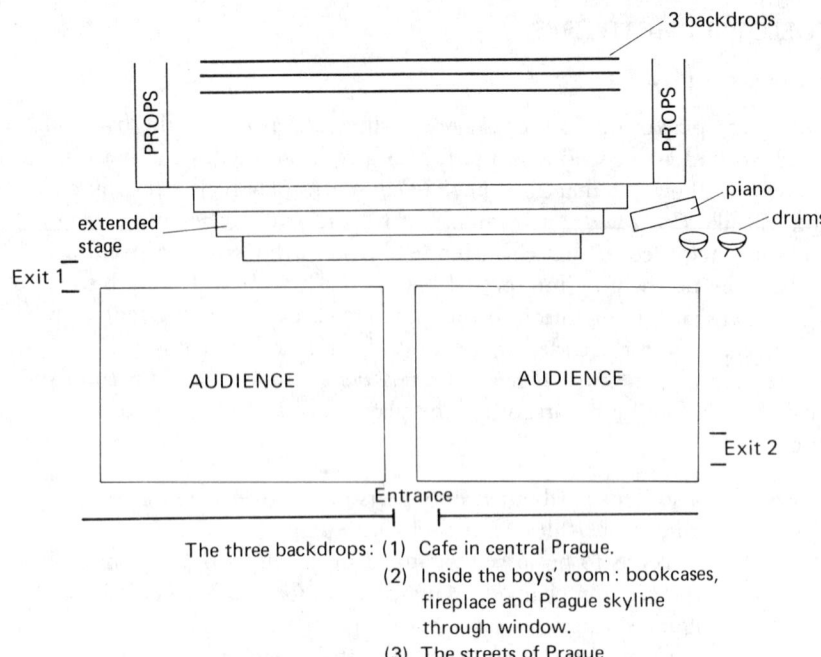

The three backdrops: (1) Cafe in central Prague.
                     (2) Inside the boys' room: bookcases, fireplace and Prague skyline through window.
                     (3) The streets of Prague

Here is another theatre plan.

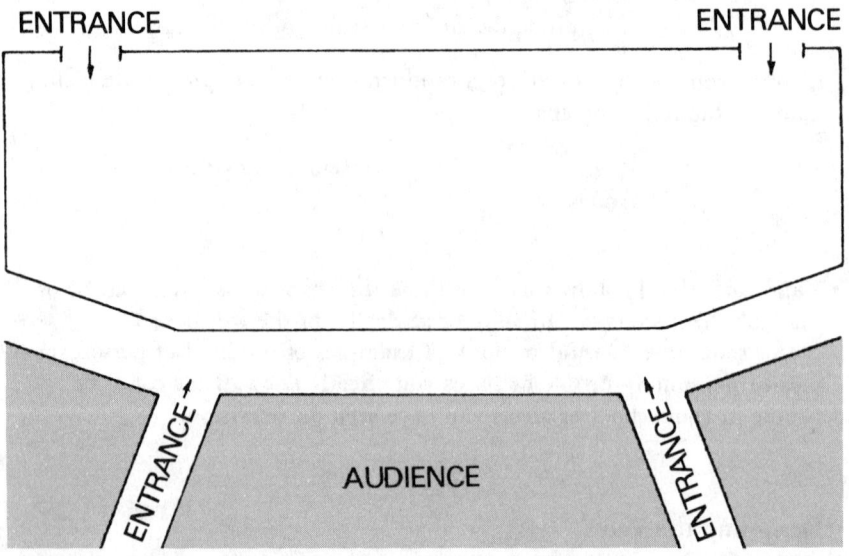

Can you design a set for *Czechmate* to fit this theatre? If you have a theatre, stage or drama room in your school, design a set to fit your space.

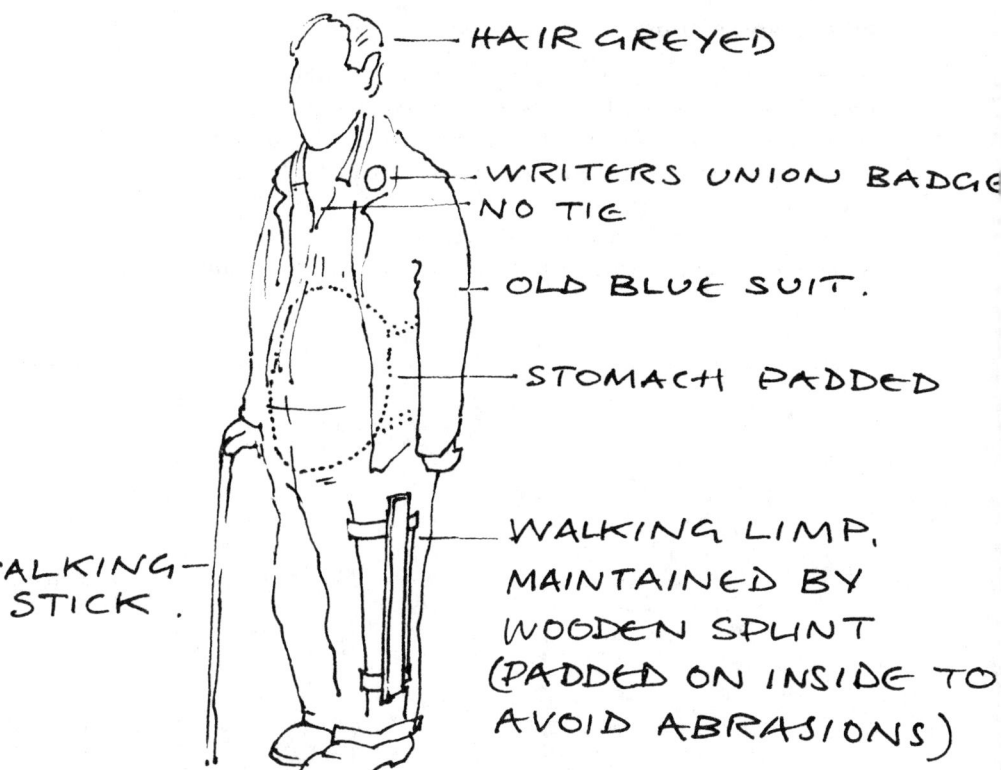

HAIR GREYED

WRITERS UNION BADGE
NO TIE

OLD BLUE SUIT.

STOMACH PADDED

WALKING—
STICK .

WALKING LIMP,
MAINTAINED BY
WOODEN SPLINT
(PADDED ON INSIDE TO
AVOID ABRASIONS)

Designing the costumes

Here is how the costume designer working on *Czechmate* planned the costume of the old journalist, Paul. She has drawn a picture of what she was hoping Paul might look like. She also wrote some notes about the effect she was trying to achieve and some of the details of the costume.

It is very often the small details that make a costume 'work', especially for plays set in our own times.

Select one or two characters from *Czechmate* and design a costume for each. Try to make up some sketches. You do not have to be able to draw, although it helps. You could find examples of the clothes you are thinking of in magazines or books. On the whole, students in Prague at this time wore the same kind of clothes as students in England.

For some characters you will need to do more than one design because they change their costume during the play.

Make notes on the details: e.g. jewellery, badges, ties, etc. You could include a few scraps of material to give an idea of what the clothes would be made of.

Editing and cutting

A play is not like a novel, which is completely finished when it is printed. Because a play has to be interpreted by the director and the actors, it is always changing. A playscript is a working document and the writer, the director and the actors all have a right to change it if they really think it necessary.

Here is an original version of the scene on page 56 of *Czechmate* in which the students decide that one of them must commit suicide as a protest.

(Vic and Val enter along with the girls. Depression hangs over them. Mark moves to catch Vic first)

Mark   Vic - Zarnak - he's on the streets - He's

Val   Oh no!

Vic   That's all I need

Jan   Vic - everyone, sit down.   Vic, remember what we agreed last night? The human protest?   We must go ahead.   NOW - today - if we wait - we won't.

Anna   You mean - suicide?

Laura   Take your own life?

Vic   Why not?   The people must be stirred!   We must show everyone that Czechoslovakia is NOT dead.   We must shame them into action.

Mark   Would you go through with it?

Vic   Yes!

Jiri   Yes!

Jan   Yes!

Val   I would too if (she almost says 'Vic')

Peter   Then we draw lots.   Whoever picks number 1 does it - goes first - for Czechoslovakia!   Give me a pen.

    (He writes down a few numbers on a piece of paper and puts them in a cap)

    Are you "in" Mark   (Mark shakes his head)

    Margarite?   (She shakes her head)

Margarite   You're just being silly

Vic   We'll see

Compare this with the final version as it appears in this script. Can you suggest why this scene was changed in this way?

Are there any scenes in the play which do not sound right to you? Find a section of a scene which you think could be improved and make notes of the changes you think are necessary.

Read your version to someone else. Does he or she agree that you have improved it?

Are there any sections of the play that you think should be cut out? Decide where your cuts would be and make notes on why you want to cut those lines out. Imagine you will have to explain to the authors why you want to cut the play (they spent a lot of time and effort writing those lines, so the reasons had better be good!)

Staging the play

The director needs to plan each scene very carefully. Not only will he plan the actions and the movements, but he will also have a general view of what the scene should look like and the effect it will have on the audience.

To do this he needs to ask himself a series of questions:

(1) From which entrance will each character come on and what position should he or she take up on the stage?

(2) At what points will each character move and how?

(3) Which objects and props need to be where during the scene?

(4) How can I be sure that the audience understands what is going on in this scene?

(5) How will I make the scene achieve its intended effect, e.g. funny or sad or exciting, etc?

(6) What do I expect from the actors in this scene?

Here is a page from the director's script:

Scene 3   *Enter with mammoth amount of noise – surround the tank*

21 August 1968

Wenceslas Square in the centre of Prague. Soviet tanks in obvious evidence.
The people in the streets are angry and vociferous. One tank is in the centre
of the stage, manned by a Russian Gunner.

shouting, yelling, cursing (not bad language)

Woman 1   What are you doing here? Get that monster out of my city.

Woman 2   Shame on you – we are peace-loving people – go home.   *Keep the noise level up.*

          (the gathering crowd grows ever more menacing.)

Man 1   Get going, Russki, we want to be Czech and Slovak, not Russian.

Man 2   (baring his chest to the tank gun)   Come on then, blow Czech
          socialism away.   *don't ever let silence reign – not even for a second.*

Russian
Gunner   (looking perplexed) But we have been sent to save you, Comrade,
          from subversion.

Women   Where is this subversion? You see only Czechs. Czechs who wish
          to be Czechs. Show me evidence of disruption in Prague, come on,
          show me!   *derision – screams, shouts of angry contempt*

Russian
Gunner   (embarrassed) We have orders!

Man 1   Stuff your orders – give us the right to be ourselves. We want
          Dubcek; he is a good leader.   *almost violent, near hysteria*

Crowd   Yes, we want Dubcek (begin to chant) – *Victor gives cue to chant*

          Dubcek!   Dubcek!   We want Dubcek.   *Do NOT stand in ranks –*
          Dubcek!   Dubcek!   We want Dubcek.   *spread out*
          Go home! Go home! Go home Russki.
          Go home! Go home! Go home Russki.

          Volume towards audience

Pick one of the scenes listed below and work out how you would stage it
on the set you have designed. (If you have not designed a set, look back
at page 64 and use the drawing of the original stage plan.)

Practise making notes like those on the page above.

(1)   Act One, Scene 2: the scene in which the students are brought
      before Zarnak (pages 9-11).
(2)   Act Two, Scene 1: the scene in which Victor is confronted by Paul
      and Emil (pages 36-9).
(3)   Act Two, Scene 7: the funeral requiem (pages 59-60).
(4)   Act Two, Scene 5: the scene which switches between the Russian
      High Command and the boys' room (pages 48-51).

Questions asked by the cast

During rehearsals, the play will be discussed in great depth by the actors and the director. The director is expected to have an opinion on most aspects of the play and will have to answer many of the questions asked by the actors.

Here are some of the questions asked by the actors working on *Czechmate*. How would you have answered them if you were the director?

Victor
'What kind of relationship do I have with Valerie at the start of the play?'

'What is most important to me, my career, my politics or my love life?'

Valerie
'At times I am confused and feeble, at other times I am very articulate. I'm not very consistent. Do you think that's realistic?'

'Do you think that I would go with Victor readily at the end of the play? It doesn't really seem to match up with the rest of my character.'

Peter
'Am I supposed to be the leader of the group or not? I seem to make all the decisions but Victor's the most politically aware.'

Paul
'Do I have *any* sympathy with the students and what they want?'

'What is my opinion of the liberal changes? Am I for or against Dubcek?'

Zarnak
'What sort of a man am I? Am I an unsophisticated bully-boy or do I really believe in what I am doing? How should I play the scene with the three students?'

If you were given one of the following parts, can you think of the questions you might ask the director?

Jan
The Editor, Emil
Lisa

When you have worked out the questions you could give them to someone else who could try to answer them.

Writing about the play

The follow-up work on the previous pages has concentrated on the process of presenting this play to an audience. Anyone who has worked on all the exercises is sure to have thought about the play in considerable depth. Any of these exercises could provide the basis for a longer piece of writing.

In school, however, it is often necessary to produce a longer piece of critical writing because that is the kind of writing examiners will be interested in. Here are four essay titles on *Czechmate* on which to base a formal piece of writing about the play:

(1) What, in your opinion, was the best way for Czech students to respond to the Russian invasion of their country? Bear in mind that there was never any doubt that the Russians could overwhelm any organised military resistance.

(2) What do the songs add to *Czechmate*? Discuss the effect of songs in a play with a serious, historical theme. What do the lyrics add to the message of the play?

(3) The role of women in *Czechmate*. Write about the way women are represented in this play. To what extent do they have a positive role to play? How would you set about adapting the play for a group of actors in which there were many more women than men?

(4) The 'Two thousand words': to print or not to print? Trace the argument that occurs in the Newspaper Office over whether or not to publish the 'Two thousand words'. (Look at the extract from the actual document on page 00 and consider the arguments in Paul's song.) Given that after the Russian take-over most of the signatories were persecuted, do you agree with Paul that the 'Two thousand words' was an empty gesture?

'Two thousand words'

The 'Two thousand words' was an open letter addressed to 'workers, farmers, officials, artists, scholars, scientists, technicians, and everyone' and was published on 27 June 1968 in four Czechoslovak newspapers. It was signed by seventy Czechoslovaks, including members of the Academy of Sciences, heads of university faculties, scientists and university professors, farmers and agronomists, actors and artists, writers and poets, doctors, lawyers, film producers, technicians, factory workers and leading sportsmen, such as Colonel Emil Zatopek, the Olympic running champion and gold medallist. Here are three extracts from the 'Two thousand words'.

'At this moment of hope, albeit hope still threatened, we turn to you. It took several months before many of us believed it was safe to speak up; many of us do not think it safe even yet. But speak up we did, and we exposed ourselves so far that we have no choice but to complete our plan to humanize the regime. If we did not, the old forces would take a cruel revenge. We turn above all to those who so far have only waited. The time now approaching will decide the issue for years to come.'

'Under dreary-looking headlines a hard battle is being reflected in the press – the battle of democracy versus soft jobs. The workers . . . can intervene in this battle by electing the right people to managements and works councils. And . . . they can help themselves best by electing as their trade union representatives natural leaders, able and honourable men without regard to party affiliation.

Though one cannot at present expect more of the central political bodies, it is urgent to achieve more at district and community level. Let us demand the departure of people who abused their power, damaged public property, acted dishonourably or brutally. Ways must be found of bringing them to resign. To mention a few: public criticism, resolutions, demonstrations, collections to buy presents for them on their retirement, strike and picketing at their front doors. But we should reject any illegal, indecent or boorish methods, which they would exploit to bring influence to bear on Alexander Dubcek. Our aversion to the writing of rude letters must be expressed so completely that the only explanation for any such missives in future would be that their recipients had ordered them themselves.'

'This spring a great opportunity came to us again, as it came after the end of the war. Again we have the chance to take into our own hands our common cause – which for working purposes we call socialism – and give it a form more appropriate to our once good reputation, and to that fairly good opinion we originally had of ourselves. The spring is over and will never return. By winter we shall know all.'

72

Light Up Your Life

(♩=132)

Eb   Eb 7 (maj)

Now they've put out the lights, We're sup -

Cm   Eb   Ab   Bb

posed to take fright, Crawl back in - to our

Eb   Fm7   Bb

We're just emp-ty heads, who ought to

Eb   Eb 7 (maj)   Cm   Bb   Eb

be in bed,— Not speak-ing our minds, they presume.

Ab   Fm7

Well, are you gon-na make it, Or

Eb   Eb 7 (maj)   Cm   Cm7

lie down and take _ it, __ Let them tram-ple

A♮7   Bb   Ab

all o-ver us? _ Are we in the right, Is it

Eb   Cm   Ab   Bb   Eb

worth a stand-up fight, Or don't you want an - y fuss?

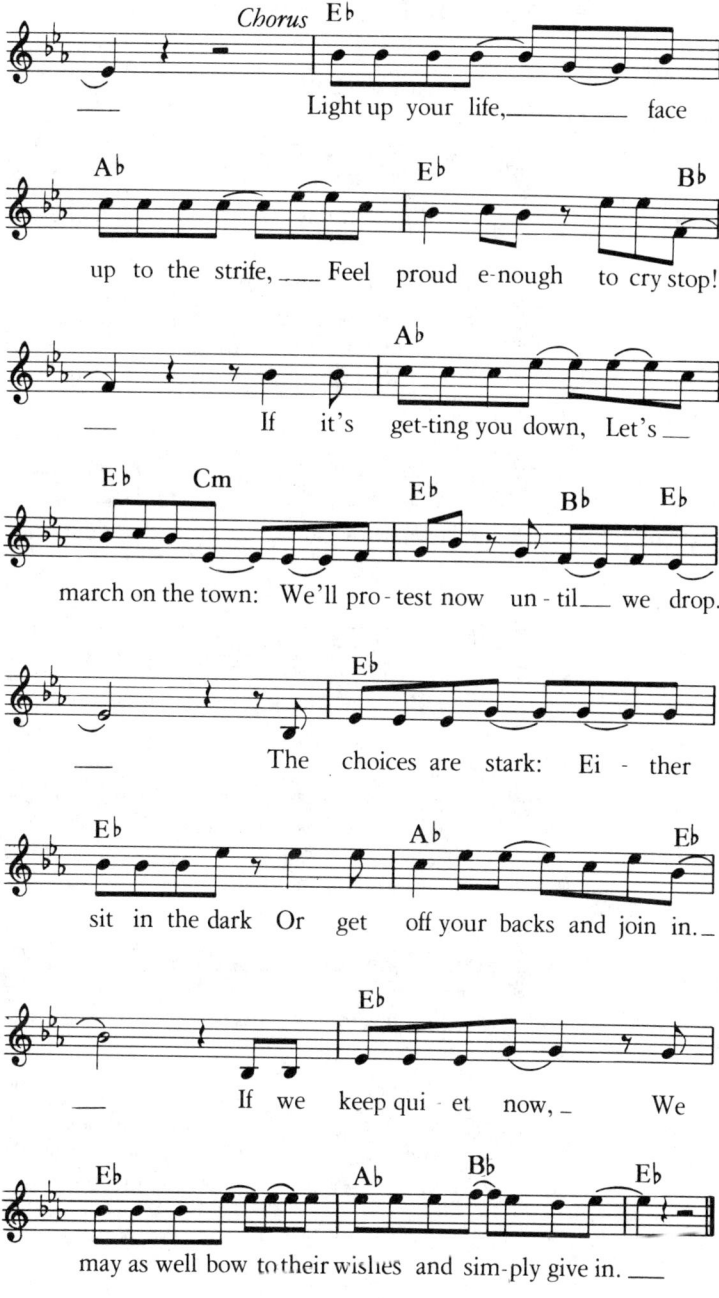

Light up your life,_____ face up to the strife,___ Feel proud e-nough to cry stop! If it's get-ting you down, Let's __ march on the town: We'll pro-test now un-til__ we drop. The choices are stark: Ei-ther sit in the dark Or get off your backs and join in._ If we keep qui-et now,_ We may as well bow to their wishes and sim-ply give in. __

Try to Tell a Teenager

Hope

Moderate (♩ = 84)

Hope, the bud-ding spring flow'r as it rush-es out to

bloom, And the chee-ry faced young school-boy barg-ing out from the class-

room, Grows a-gain in-side our hearts, fills our ev'-ry wak-ing.

hour, Let-ting dreams of how it might be warm our sen-ses with false

pow'r; While our heart beat quick-ens dai-ly, and our step has rais'd its

pace, And there's spar-kle in your bright eyes, a flush u-pon your

face. May it be so, may it be so___

don't stop now. Go the whole way,___

He's a Hero

Fast (♩ =156)

Theres a wild ___ gleam in her eye,___

Ev' - ry line ___ ends with a sigh,___ She sees just him, ___

no one else ___ gets ___ through.___ Does he walk ___ or

does he glide? ___ Oh to be ___ there ___ by his side: ___ A

God to her, ___ though mere - ly man ___ to ___ you. ___

Do you think she's may - be dim ___ To see an - y - thing

___ in him? ___ Per - haps we ought ___ to take her to the vet.

___ Yes, a doc - tor ___ is no use; ___ She'd

only give him_ mad a - buse, For there's real - ly on - ly one man in her _ life._

Chorus

And he's a He - ro,_ can't you un - der - stand? A He - ro, _ is - n't it just grand? Ev' - ry - thing_ he does, he does_ with style, _ For he's her He - ro,_ Mis - ter Al - ways Right. A He - ro,_ such a love - ly sight;_ I won - der what it's like to be _ so _ fine; _ For me I'm glad_ he'll ne - ver_ be_ all mine._

Mr Newsman

Moderate (♪=144)

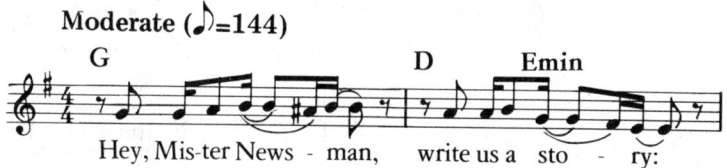

Hey, Mis-ter News - man, write us a sto - ry:

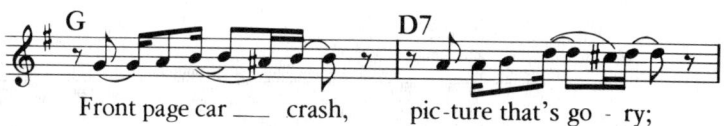

Front page car ___ crash, pic-ture that's go - ry;

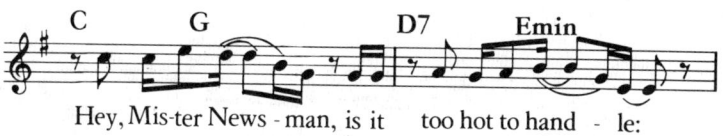

Hey, Mis-ter News - man, is it too hot to hand - le:

Gov-ern -ment foul - up, po -li - ti-cal scan-dal?

Hey, Mis-ter News - man, rake in the dirt, Make a

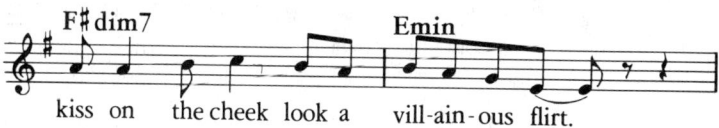

kiss on the cheek look a vill-ain-ous flirt.

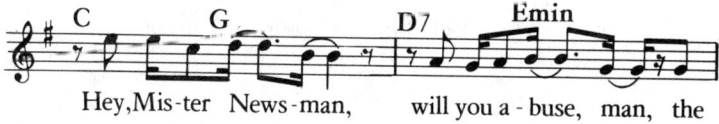

Hey, Mis-ter News -man, will you a - buse, man, the

pow'r of the press? Care-ful as you go,___ man,

can't be the cause of the Par - ty's dis - tress.

Chorus

How did you do it, did you have to work hard?

Or did you take the eas - y way___ with the

Par-ty's ma - gic card?

Have you sold out all___ your friends, do we

now all have _ to bow?

Will you re-port our meet-ings? Tell us right now.

Left Alone

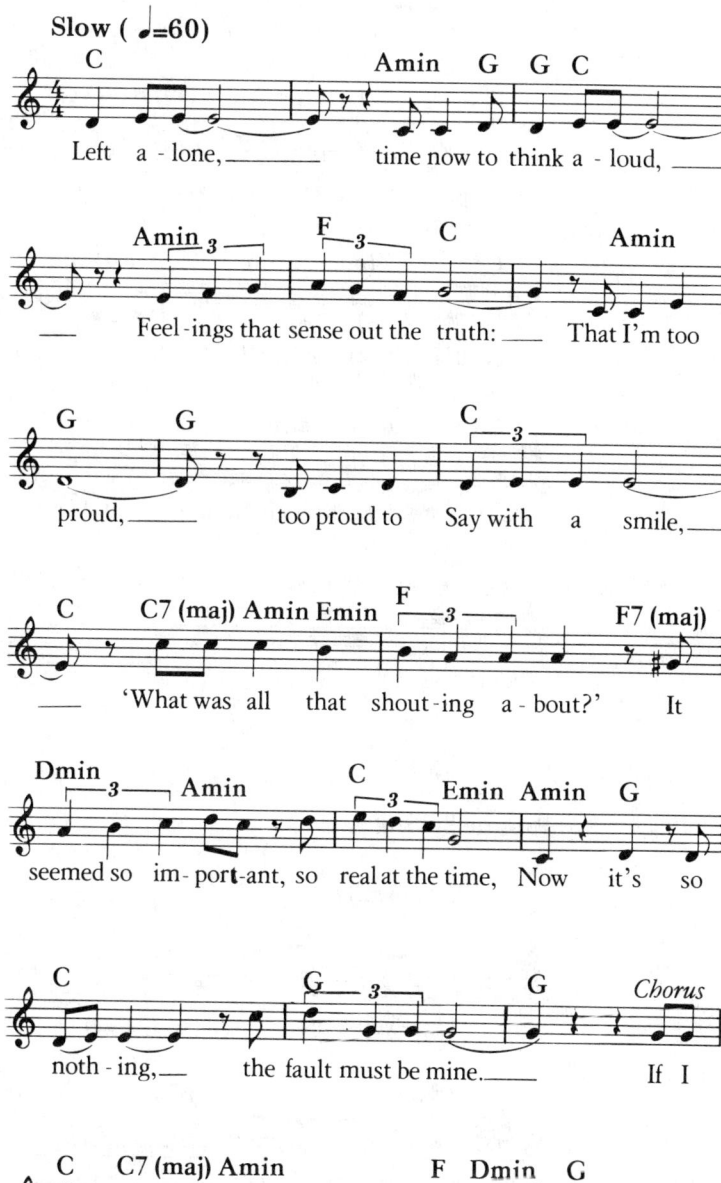

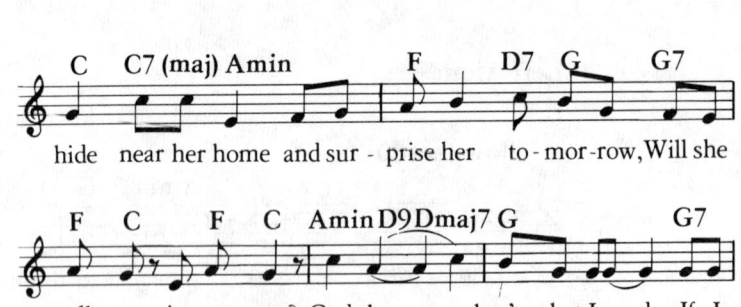

C C7 (maj) Amin   F   D7   G   G7

hide near her home and sur - prise her to - mor-row, Will she

F   C   F   C   Amin D9 Dmaj7 G   G7

walk past, ig-nore me? God knows,_ that's what I need. If I

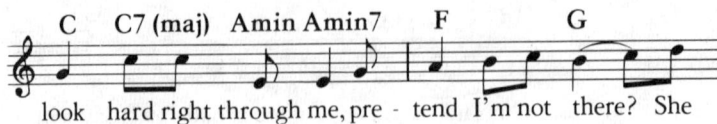

C   C7 (maj) Amin   F Dmin   G   G7

say it's all my fault, If I   buy her some flow'rs, Will she

C   C7 (maj) Amin Amin7   F   G

look hard right through me, pre - tend I'm not there? She

C   G Amin7 Emin   F C Dmin7 G11 C

should, yes I know it, but   please,_____   I do care._

Prague Spring

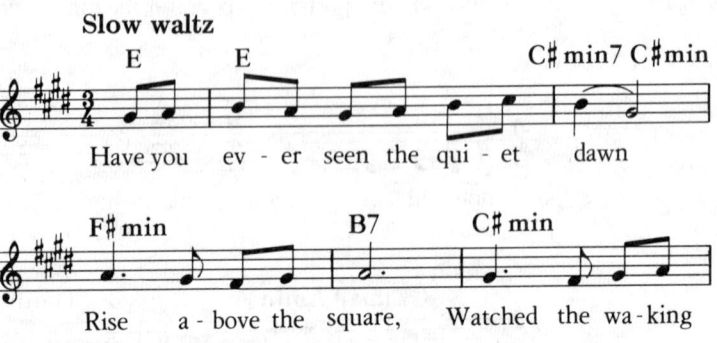

Slow waltz

E   E   C♯ min7 C♯min

Have you ev - er seen the qui - et   dawn

F♯ min   B7   C♯ min

Rise   a - bove the square, Watched the wa - king

C♯min7   **F♯maj**   **B7**

morn spread With   si - lent ten-der care,

E   **F♯min7 C♯min**

Felt the first ray touch your heart,   Sud - den-ly a -

B   **C♯min**   **C♯min7**

ware The new day's come, what's passed is gone, Prague

F♯maj7   **B G♮7 B7** *Chorus* **C**   **C7 (maj)**

spring is ev'-ry-where? It's so   won-der-ful to be a -

Amin   **G**   **Emin** **Amin**   **Amin7**

live on a morn-ing like this,   Won-der-ful to hold your

F♯min7 Emaj7   **G7**   **Bmaj7 C**   **C7(maj)**

hand, dare to steal a kiss; Where else can you dance and

Amin   **G**   **G7**   **Emin7**

waltz   In   the   mid - dle of the   street,

Amin   **Amin7** **F♯min7 Bmaj7**   **Emin**

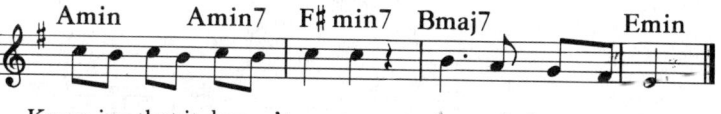

Know-ing that it does-n't mat-ter who you chance to meet?

Two Thousand Words

Fairly fast (♩=144)

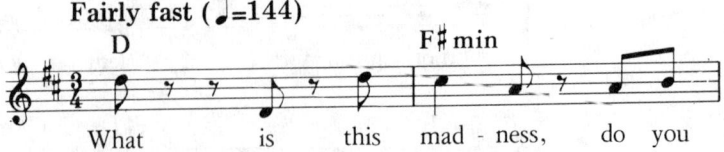

What is this mad - ness, do you

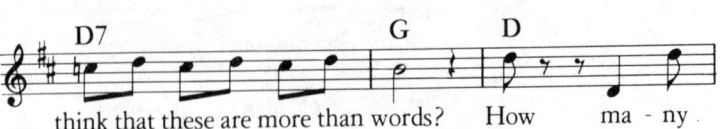

think that these are more than words? How ma - ny

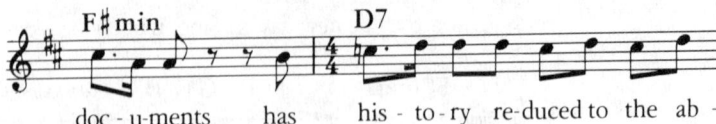

doc - u - ments has his - to - ry re - duced to the ab -

surd? I thought you were in - tell - i - gent, the cream of

stu - dent - hood; You bring me this as though it's

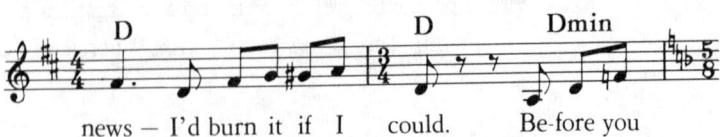

news — I'd burn it if I could. Be - fore you

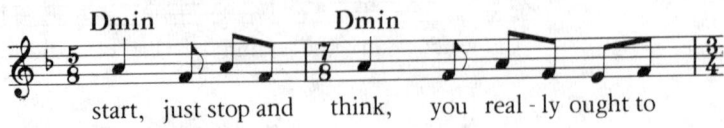

start, just stop and think, you real - ly ought to

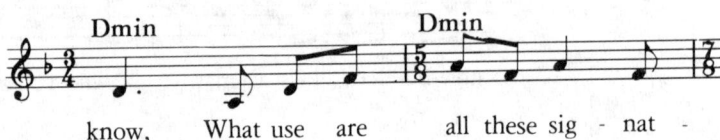

know, What use are all these sig - nat -

ures be-fore an i-ron foe? Will pro-

fess - ors and cler - gy-men, re -

port - ers or stu - dents, Or all the

Work - ers' Coun - cils be ab - le to pre -

vent The kind of right - eous an - ger which de -

lights our Mos - cow friends And gives them

am - ple rea-son to strike and make a-mends? You

seem to think me weak and scared be -

86

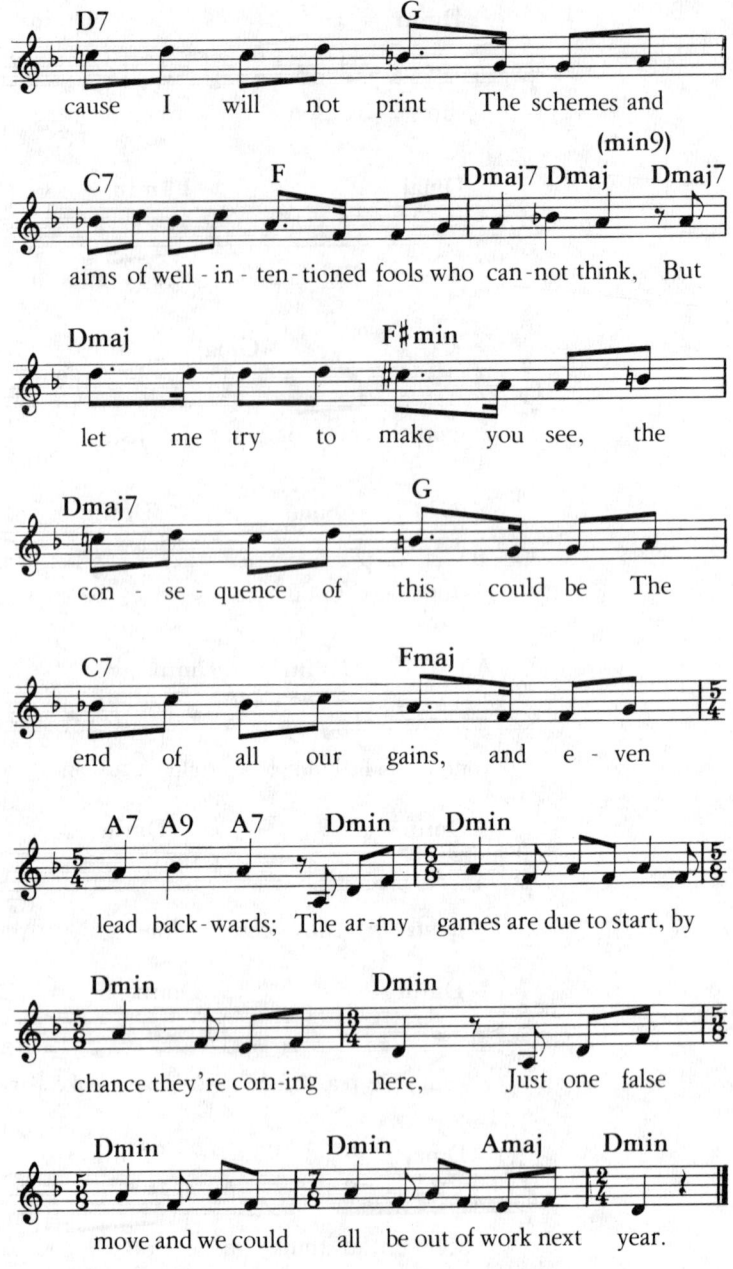

Go Home Russki

Fast (♩=116)

C♯min

You're not want-ed here,
car-rions of fear,

C♯min (maj7)

C♯min (min7)

F♯maj

can't you sense our dis-gust? __ To your

F♯min

C♯m

of-fer of tanks, Dub-cek ans-wered 'No thanks',

E♭7
3

A♭(6♯)

That e-ven *you* could have sussed.

C♯min

C♯min (maj7)

Where are the trait-ors, or Com-mun-ist bait-ers?__ It's

C♯min (min7)

F♯maj

C♯min

plain to see___ they do not ex-ist.__ Your

C♯min Gmaj

Gmin

E♭ maj

miss-ion's a lie,___ you can-not de-ny,___

A7

D7

Chorus

B7

we greet you here with raised fist.__ So,

C♯min / **Emaj**

Go home Russ - ki__ back to the Vol - ga;

C♯min / **G♯7**

Go home Russ - ki put a - way your re-vol - ver;__

C♯min / **Emaj**

Go home Russ - ki__ take your tanks back;

C♯min / **G♯7** / **C♯min**

Go home and stay there __ that's all we ask.__

Calling the Free World

Fast (♩=115)

Dm / **A7** / **Dm**

Call-ing the free world from Ra-di-o Prague: The

Gm / **Dm**

tanks have ta - ken o - ver from our trams;

Am / **Gm** / **Dm**

They roam the streets like packs of dogs, _

C / **Dm** / **A7** / **Dm** / **Slower**

Pro - tec-ting us from free - dom's wrongs, And

D / **Dm** / **a tempo**

dan - ger - ous de - moc - ra - cy;

Call-ing the free world, can you hear___ me?_

Lis-ten to us now, it's Ra-di-o Prague: Our

lead-ers have been ta-ken in-to care,

And Russ-ian iron clanks o-min-ous threats,

Deaf to pro-tests, tears or wrath;

We must be saved, they say.

Call-ing the free world, can you act to-day?

If an-y-one's out___ there, it's

Ra-di-o Prague: The ci-ty does-n't want to lose its

soul; All we ask is the right to be our-selves,

Not strip our minds our hearts, our homes;

We must con-form, they say. Call-ing the free world, can't you

keep them at bay? Hear us while you can, it's

Ra - di - o Prague: So much has hap-pened to us o-ver night;

The prom-ised dawn of Dub-cek's new re-forms Has

fa - ded in - to dark - er back-ward ways;

Change is not a word that Mos-cow will bear.

Call - ing the free world, do you real - ly care?

The Fool's Song

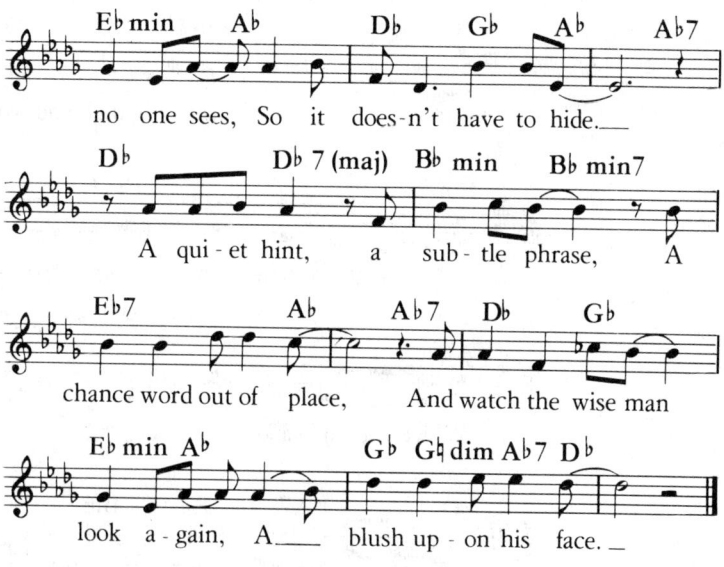

no one sees, So it does-n't have to hide.___

A qui - et hint, a sub - tle phrase, A

chance word out of place, And watch the wise man

look a - gain, A___ blush up - on his face. _

In Childhood Fantasy

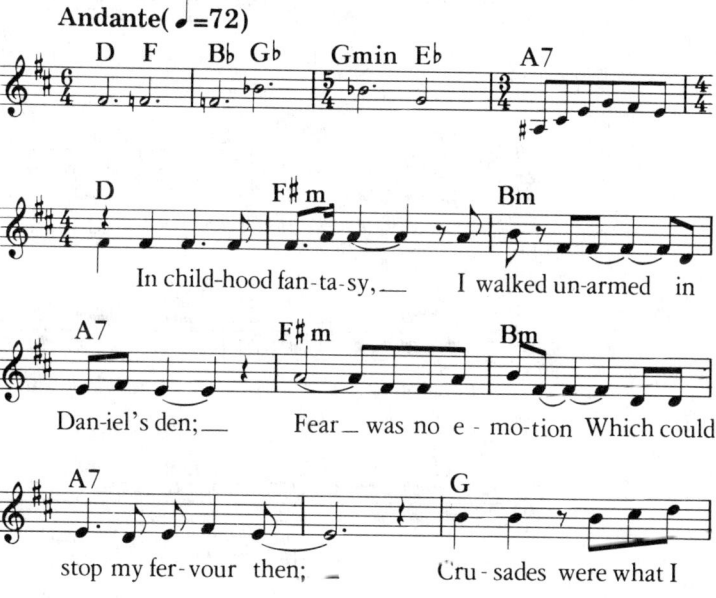

In child-hood fan-ta-sy,___ I walked un-armed in

Dan-iel's den;___ Fear___ was no e - mo-tion Which could

stop my fer-vour then; _ Cru - sades were what I

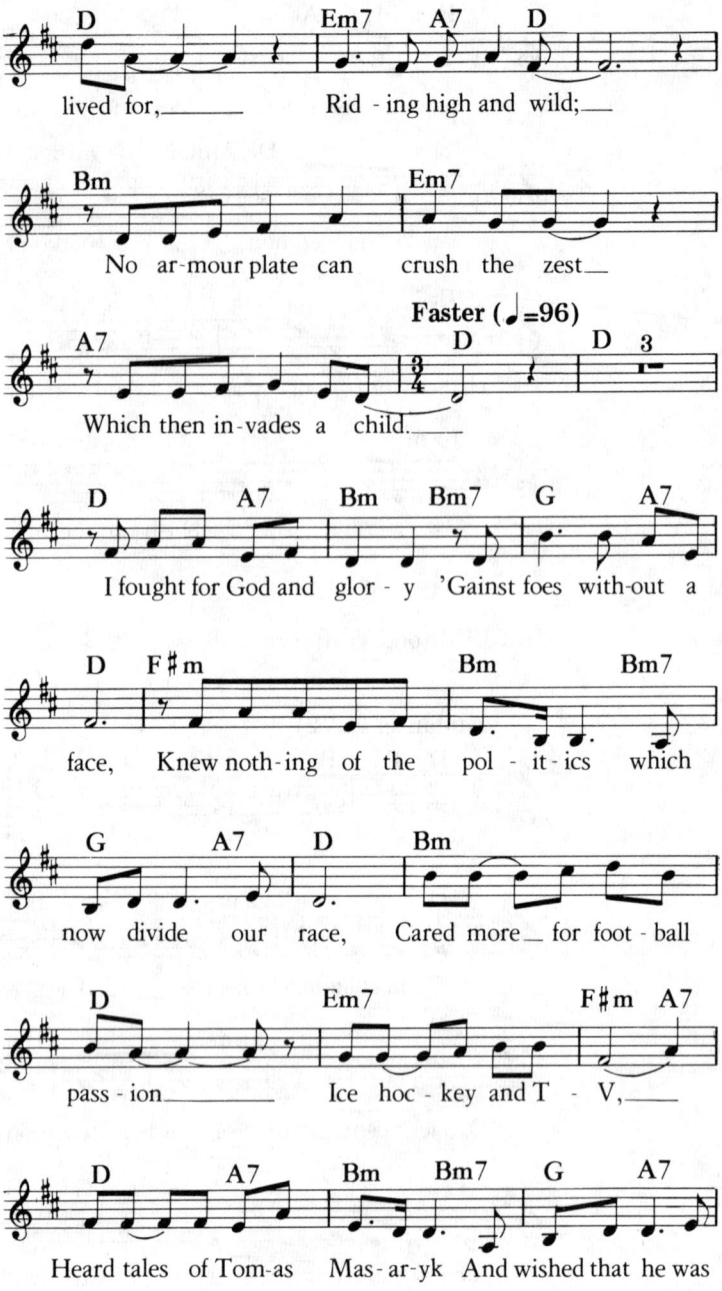

lived for,____ Rid - ing high and wild;___

No ar-mour plate can crush the zest__

Faster (♩ =96)

Which then in-vades a child.____

I fought for God and glor - y 'Gainst foes with-out a

face, Knew noth-ing of the pol - it - ics which

now divide our race, Cared more__ for foot - ball

pass - ion_____ Ice hoc - key and T - V,___

Heard tales of Tom-as Mas-ar-yk And wished that he was

land? My life? Who's heard of Jan?

And if I do, will ev-'ry-one dub me a

mad - man? Some-one, some-where must raise his voice,

Stand up and act right now;__ Must it be me? Why

not? Why not? I free-ly took that vow __

($\mathbf{\downarrow}$=72)

Will an-y-one re-mem-ber me? Will death re-lease my

soul? Will Czech and Slo-vak take a stance, make

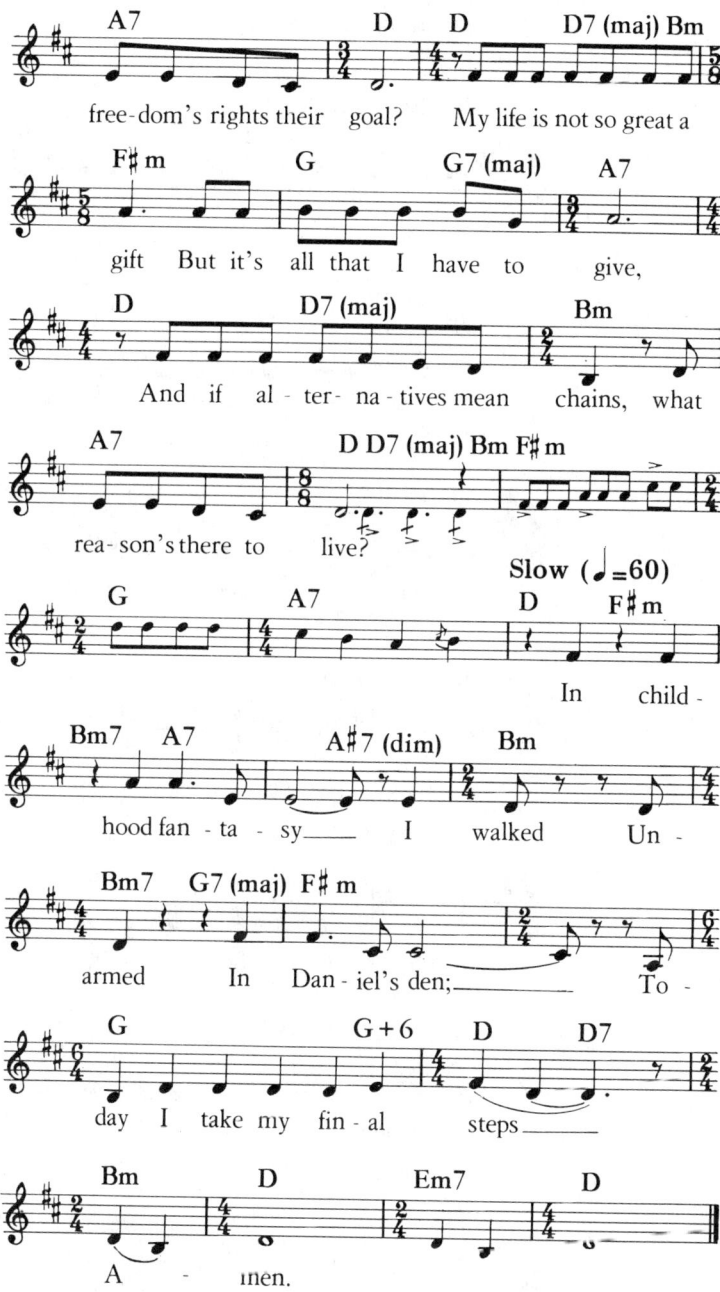

free-dom's rights their goal? My life is not so great a

gift But it's all that I have to give,

And if al - ter - na - tives mean chains, what

rea - son's there to live?

Slow (♩=60)

In child -

hood fan - ta - sy____ I walked Un -

armed In Dan - iel's den;____ To -

day I take my fin - al steps____

A - men.

Requiem at Jan's funeral

Re-qui-em ae - ter-nam do-na e -is

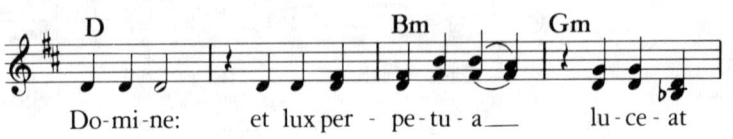

Do-mi-ne: et lux per - pe-tu - a___ lu - ce - at

e - is. Te de-cet hym - nus, De - us in

Si - on: et ti - bi re - de-tur vo-tum in Je -

ru - sa-lem; Ex-au-di o - ra- ti - o - nem

me - am, ad te - om-nis ca - ro___

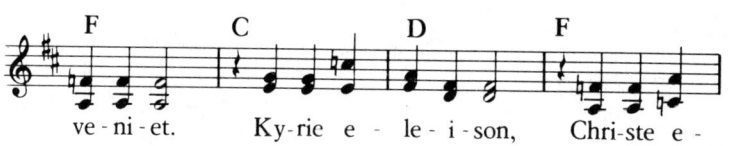

ve - ni - et.　　Ky-rie　e　-　le - i - son,　　Chri-ste　e -

le - i - son,　　Ky-rie　e　-　le - i - son.　　A -

men.

Jan's Song

Fast (♩=132)

live on Jan,____ live on Jan.____

Though you're first in the draw, did you think it a raw

deal. As you poised to pro - test?_ Was there fear__ in your

breast? I ne - ver thought that you real - ly would do such a

thing. But you stood as a light _ 'Gainst the Russ - ian might.

When the last au - tumn leaf _ falls free in re - lief, you re -

main; Though the Par - ty de - nies,_ you're a - live _ in our

eyes. In giv - ing your life _ to high - light our strife a - gainst

force, You stood out a - lone _ Russ - ki go home!

Repeat Chorus then repeat Requiem

Czechmate was first performed at Alva Academy on 18 June 1980, with the following cast:

PETER	Gordon Hyde
JIRI	David Foster
ANNA	Sandra Forsyth
LAURA	Jennifer Dunk
MARGARITE	Barbara Tainsh
VICTOR	Roddy Hunter
VALERIE	Carol Rae
JAN	Stan Calder
MARK	Henry Conroy
JOHAN	Alec MacDonald
PAUL	Allan Heggie
EDITOR (EMIL)	Colin Aitken
TOMAS	Anthony Duffy
PRIEST	Chris Clark
LISA	Susie Gilchrist
BREADWOMAN	Morag Calder
ZARNAK	Colin Aitken
WPC	Lorraine Kerr
VISCLAV	Gregor Paterson
STARNAK	David Donaldson
GUNNER	Robin Morton
SOLDIER 1	Douglas Muir
SOLDIER 2	David Wilson
COMMANDER	Gillian Ramage
MAJOR	Ian MacMillan